Stress

Joe Macdonald Wallace

The Crowood Press

First published in 1988 by
The Crowood Press
Ramsbury, Marlborough,
Wiltshire SN8 2HE

© Joe Macdonald Wallace 1988

All rights reserved. No part of this publication may be
reproduced or transmitted in any form or by any means,
electronic or mechanical, including photocopy, recording,
or any information storage and retrieval system, without
permission in writing from the publishers.

British Library Cataloguing in Publication Data

Wallace, J. Macdonald (Joseph Macdonald), *1918 –*
    Stress: a practical guide to coping.
        1. Man. Stress
            I. Title
            155.9

ISBN 1 85223 059 2

Line illustrations by Claire Upsdale-Jones

Dedicated to Robert Earl Rinehart MD, a good friend
who helped to found the ISTCS, and who dedicated his
life to the alleviation of the pains of rheumatic diseases.

Typeset by Q-Set, 2 Conway Road, Hucclecote, Gloucester
Printed in Great Britain at The Bath Press

Contents

Introduction

The International Stress and Tension Control Society is a registered charity, a multidisciplinary organisation of professionals who are concerned with stress research and stress management in many countries. The President of the Society is Professor F.J. McGuigan, Director of the Institute of Stress Management at the United States International University in San Diego, California. President of the United Kingdom Branch is Dr Desmond Kelly, an eminent psychiatrist and Medical Director of the Priory Hospital in London; President of the French branch is Dr Suzanne Masson, a physician and Professor of Psychomotricité at the University of Paris. Current Vice-Presidents of the Society are Dr Yves Chesni, a psychiatrist from Brittany, Dr Desmond Kelly, and Marian Showers, a physical therapist from Portland, Oregon.

My role in the Society is as one of the founders, and as Director responsible for developing the Society outside the American continent. Because the Society is multidisciplinary, there are many different viewpoints amongst its members on how stress can be managed, and even on what is stress. It is unlikely that all members would agree with what is contained in this book, or even with the way in which it is expressed. Fortunately, the book, based on courses I have conducted and developed over many years, is not aimed at those who are already experts in the field, advanced into realms far beyond the scope of these chapters.

My own professional life has been for thirty years as a teacher of health education and physical education in universities and institutes of higher education, and subsequently as a consultant in stress management in universities, colleges, hospitals and management training centres in twelve different countries. I am an educator, not a therapist, so that this book is to be seen as a contribution to health education, not as a kind of pseudo-therapy.

I have tried to write it to be of interest to intelligent men and women who are constantly hearing about or reading about stress, but are not very sure what it is all about. The emphasis is not just

4

on what stress is, but also on how to manage one's own stress. Throughout the book it is constantly repeated that stress management is something that you do for yourself, not something that is done to you, or for you: it is a psychomotor skill to be learned. The pattern of successful learning of any complex psychomotor skill has four parts – understanding, training, practice and application.

My responsibility is to provide the understanding and the training in stress management. This I try to do in the text of each chapter, and in the practical lesson at the end of each chapter. The practice and the application are the responsibility of the reader. Fortunately, the practice of this skill is never just an addition to life's chores. It is always a pleasant experience.

This is not a book to be picked up, read in a few hours, then forgotten. Read it leisurely over a couple of months, one chapter per week. The reading of each chapter does not take long, but the practice of each lesson should be done every day for a week, gradually building up your own skill. Books usually begin at chapter one, but this one is different. Start at chapter eight, and complete the inventory there, so that you have some measure of your own stress level before you begin your training in the first chapter.

Wherever masculine gender is used, it is meant to include feminine gender, with some exceptions, where only one gender is relevant.

Whatever errors are to be found, they are all my own. For what is good, I am indebted to many people, some of whom are mentioned in the text, including the late Dr Arthur Steinhaus, Dr Edmund Jacobson, Dr Hans Selye; to Dr Desmond Kelly, who pointed me towards this book; to Donna Jean and the late Jack Claypole, who never got round to publishing their joint masterpiece; and to the many thousands of students who have helped me, over the years, to understand that stress, if properly managed, can be a great aid to better living.

I am grateful for the patience and help of my wife, Josephine, on whom many additional domestic burdens fell as I became immersed in the writing.

J.M.W
Rottingdean, Sussex 1988

1
Understanding Stress

Writing over 2,000 years ago, the Greek historian Herodotus described how, in the mighty city of Babylon, there were no doctors. When someone suffered from a severe illness which showed no signs of improving, the family laid him on a stretcher on the bridge which crossed the great river Euphrates. Any traveller crossing the bridge was obliged by law to stop and enquire about the symptoms of the disease. If he had previously observed similar symptoms in any other person who had recovered, the traveller was then obliged to recount the method of the cure to the invalid and his family. Herodotus gives no clue as to how successful was this ancient state method of health and social security, but presumably it fitted well with the natural laws of the great healer Time, and many wonderful cures were recorded.

In modern times, no one need be at a loss for advice about the illnesses he may experience. If, within the finite bounds of orthodox medical practice, the patient can find little relief and no cure, there is an unlimited army of unorthodox practitioners, some knowledgeable and well-trained, some ignorant and untrained, mountebanks, charlatans and well-meaning relatives, ready and willing to take the place of the travellers on the bridge over the Euphrates, and to supply dubious knowledge that may pass for wisdom in the receptive mind of the unfortunate invalid. This applies also in the field of stress management.

When, more than thirty years ago, at the University of Otago in New Zealand, I began to teach in the field of biological stress, there were not many people around who understood the meaning of the term, nor its significance as an important factor in health and disease. In the current decade, one can hardly open a newspaper or a magazine, or switch on the radio or the television without encountering an article or a programme on some aspect of stress. Executive stress, stress in pregnancy, occupational stress, stress in unemployment, stress in bereavement, stress in sport, stress in performance, and stress in an infinite number of other areas – all of

6

these open up avenues of expression for an eager journalist waiting for a story to turn up. And often the stories are very odd indeed. There are now numerous learned journals devoted to polysyllabic dissertations on, and investigations into, stress in all aspects of human activity. Universities, hospitals and clinics around the world have their departments or institutes for stress research or stress management.

From a very private conception, through a gestation period threatened with rejection by scientists and the untutored alike, the stress industry has finally been born, albeit with many blemishes. Supported on an often less than credible theoretical base, the exercisers, the hypnotisers, the meditators, the instrumentalists, the pill-merchants, the rubbers, the smellers, and the cassette makers have joined the academics and orthodox therapists and educators to make the general population conversant with stress. Yet it must be said that there are still not many people around who have really grasped the meaning and implications of biological stress. Even at high-level international conferences, I listen to 'experts' learnedly discuss stress without defining the term, and it is clear that what they are talking about differs markedly from the concept of stress held by many of their audience. Reading about stress in books and magazines, in newspapers, and even at times in learned journals, I often have to conclude that the author is not very clear on the concept of stress.

If, in your childhood, you read Lewis Carroll's *Alice Through The Looking Glass*, you may remember the part where Alice chides Humpty-Dumpty about his abuse of language. 'When I use a word,' replies Humpty-Dumpty firmly, 'it means just what I choose it to mean – neither more nor less.' This is sound evidence of a strong, confident, aggressive and probably mixed-up personality, but it does not contribute towards improved communication, and tends to leave the listener, or reader, in a state of confusion. Stress has become a Humpty-Dumpty term, meaning whatever the speaker or writer wants it to mean, so that a great deal of misunderstanding is sown in the minds of the general public. Even those whose professional or technical education should give them some advantage often remain unclear about what they mean when they use the term. In my work I lecture to physicians, psychologists, nurses, teachers and many other professional groups, and I have learned that I cannot presume that they all have the same concept of stress. It is rather futile to try to demonstrate how to manage a process about which we all have different ideas, so I have to begin by defining my terms. In general, the medical profession knows little about biological stress, or even rejects the concept. Few medical schools in the United Kingdom or the United States, and even fewer in other parts of the world, have time to introduce lectures on stress diseases or stress management into an already overcrowded curriculum.

When the British edition of Hans Selye's seminal book *The Stress of Life* was published in 1956, it carried a foreword by the then President of the Royal College of Physicians, who asserted that Selye's theory of stress was the most important concept in medicine since the germ theory of Pasteur. It is clear that this viewpoint has by no means been accepted as received wisdom by medical schools, and it is unlikely that many physicians who graduated more than ten years ago have any viewpoint on stress, other than that it is not a medical problem. But the climate is changing. In 1985 a stress clinic was established at the Maudsley Hospital in London, under the leadership of Dr David Wheatley, who is also the editor of a new international journal called *Stress Medicine*. Psychiatrists, at least, are beginning to take stress seriously.

Psychologists began to interest themselves in stress during the sixties and seventies, although few university courses touched on the subject at that time. Even as late as 1975, dictionaries of psychology did not include biological stress, and usually defined stress in physical terms. In recent years, the fields of stress research and stress management have tended to be dominated by psychologists, particularly those who call themselves behaviour therapists, so that stress management is often thought of as a form of therapy. This succeeds mainly in limiting its scope and effectiveness.

DEFINITIONS

If this book is to be really helpful to its readers, then I must define stress clearly and unequivocally, so that you will know without any doubt what it is I am proposing to help you manage. If you don't accept the definition, then you might as well close the book at that point, for the rest of the story will be meaningless. But before I define stress, there are two other ambiguous terms which will appear frequently in these pages, so we must be clear about these, too.

Tension

This word is frequently used to mean a state of general physiological arousal, when you feel apprehensive about some impending event. Used in this way, it is an inaccurate term. For our purposes, the definition is more simple:

Tension is the contraction of muscle fibres.
To be tense or *to tense up* means to contract muscle fibres.

Relaxation

This is another Humpty-Dumpty term meaning, at various times according to the speaker, reading a book, playing games, playing the piano or other instrument, going for a walk, or merely sitting doing nothing. But, of course, it is possible to be doing any of these things, and to be by no means relaxed. For our purposes, this definition is simple, too:

Relaxation is the elongation of muscle fibres, the opposite of *tension*.
To relax means to let muscle fibres lose any tension in them.

Obviously, if you let all your muscle fibres relax at once, you will finish up in a heap on the floor, a highly undesirable end in most situations, but, under the right conditions, to be able to let your muscle fibres relax can be very beneficial.

Stress

When I look up the meaning of *stress* in the excellent *Collins English Dictionary*, I find, amongst various definitions, that *stress* is '. . . mental, emotional or physical strain or tension'. So I turn first to *strain*, and this is defined as '. . . subjected to mental tension or stress'. Then I turn to *tension*, which is defined as '. . . mental or emotional strain;

stress'. A circular definition in each case, not really giving any clue as to how we can manage this nebulous condition.

Under the sub-heading of Physics, stress is defined as '. . . a force or system of forces producing deformation or strain.' When a train crosses a bridge, the weight of the train is stress applied to the bridge, producing deformation or strain in the timbers or girders of the bridge. If this stress is applied often enough, the deformation caused may lead to the bridge becoming unsafe, and eventually to a complete breakdown and tragedy. It is tempting to transfer this physical concept of the engineer to the human condition. Indeed, Dr Lionel Haward, Professor of Clinical Psychology at the University of Surrey, insists that they should be considered to be the same. In the human, according to this concept, many different forces press upon him from all angles – work, family, recreation, politics. Eventually, he may weaken under the stress of these forces, become less effective, perhaps become ill and, like the bridge, break down completely. This is an attractive concept, held by many to be self-evident. In my opinion, it is misleading and unhelpful when we try to find a way to manage our stress. Indeed, if someone hits you on the head with a blunt instrument, you will experience both physical stress and biological stress at the same time. So I reject this concept of physical stress and biological stress as being the same thing. They are quite different, and it is important that you grasp this difference.

DEVELOPMENT OF THE CONCEPT OF BIOLOGICAL STRESS

A major characteristic of all living things is irritability, that is, readiness to respond to a stimulus. Throughout human history, this tendency to respond to a stimulus with physiological arousal and bodily changes must have been apparent, even to the earliest type of human species. Faced by a sabre-toothed tiger or an inimical stranger, primitive man would feel his heart pounding more rapidly, his body perspiring, his muscles tensing, his hair standing up on the nape of his neck, his mouth drying up, and other changes taking place within him. Confronted by different stimuli, perhaps, the same physiological responses would be experienced by men and women of all cultures. Once the danger had passed, or been overcome, the functions of the body would quieten down again and return to normal. It is only in the past century or so that the significance of these changes in response to stimuli has been understood, and only in recent decades that we have learned how this instinctive behaviour can not only protect our lives, but also destroy us.

In the middle of the nineteenth century, Claude Bernard, Director of the prestigious Collège de France, and an experimental physiologist of renown, postulated that life can only be sustained if the internal conditions of the body are maintained within relatively small limits of variation of such functions as temperature, heart rate, blood-pressure, acidity, oxygen supply, sugar in the blood, and so on. If such functions vary too much, illness will develop, and if major variations are sustained for some time, death may result.

In 1929, in his book *Bodily Changes in Pain, Hunger, Fear and Rage*, Dr Walter B. Cannon, an American physiologist, described in great detail these many changes that take place in the body when faced with a sabre-toothed tiger, an enemy soldier, a threatening drunk, a runaway automobile, or any other stimulus. Coining a new phrase, he described these changes as preparation '. . . for fight or for flight'. In his *Wisdom of the Body*, published in 1932, Cannon showed how all the systems of the body co-operate to try to maintain the equilibrium of that which Claude Bernard had described as the '*milieu intérieur*.' Cannon coined another word, *homeostasis*, from the Greek word *homoio*, meaning the same, and the Latin word *stare*, to stand or, in the vernacular, to stay put, to express this physiological equilibrium so essential to health and to life.

Since the seminal works of Cannon and many of his contemporaries, we have had a reasonably sound knowledge of the many physiological changes that take place in the body when faced with a threatening situation or great physical exertion, but much remained to be sought out, learned, and eventually applied to understanding its influence on our lifestyles.

Hans Selye

A major contributor to this research, and to understanding the influence of our lifestyles on our homeostasis was Dr Hans Selye, an endocrinologist of Viennese origin, although his major work was done at McGill University in Canada. He has been dubbed by some as 'the father of stress', but it would probably be more accurate to say that Selye was the midwife at the birth of the concept of biological stress, and, like so many other vital discoveries in health, the birth was more accidental than intentional. Selye was a medical student at the time Cannon was pouring out his numerous research papers and books, and, at the time, probably knew little about Cannon's work. As a medical student, Selye followed the routine of clinical processions around the hospital wards, pausing at each bed while the professor explained the symptoms and syndromes of the various illnesses to the attentive band of students. As he absorbed the professorial observations, Selye noticed some common factors about all the patients, which were never mentioned by the professors. No matter which illness was present, in each patient there tended to be a rise in temperature, a change in pulse rate, a loss of appetite, a loss of interest in what was going on round about, and other symptoms. In his mind, Selye dubbed this as 'the syndrome of just being sick', as it did not appear to be related to any specific disease. As it also did not seem to be important to the omniscient professors, he did not pursue this interest, and soon forgot all about it.

Experimental Studies

After qualifying in medicine, Selye specialised in endocrinology, the study of the ductless glands of the body, and of the hormones they produce. At that time, during the twenties and thirties, only a few of the body's hormones had been discovered, and it was to the search for new types of these chemical messengers that Selye turned his mind. In the biochemistry department of McGill University, he injected extracts from cattle ovaries into rats, carefully monitoring the changes that took place, to see if any unpredictable changes could be attributed to the action of an unknown hormone. To his great satisfaction, certain changes occurred every time the extract was injected. The cortex, or outer parts of the suprarenal glands lying on top of the kidneys grew larger and very active in discharging their fatty substances into the bloodstream; the lymph glands, the thymus gland and the spleen – all parts of the immunity mechanisms of the body – shrank in size, and quite severe ulcers appeared in the stomach and digestive canal. The degree of change depended on the amount of extract injected. This, thought Selye jubilantly, was a sure sign of the action of some new hormone. Soon, however, he found that the same changes took place in the experimental rats no matter what was injected. Indeed, it was not necessary to inject anything at all. If the experimental animals were subjected to any kind of threatening stimulus – heat, cold, immobilisation, noise, constant movement, handling, and so on – the same triad of changes was found: swelling of glands on top of the kidneys; shrinkage of immunity mechanisms; and peptic ulcers. Selye's mind went back to his observation of patients during his ward rounds as a student. Could this be 'the syndrome of just being sick'?

As the investigations continued, the physiological changes taking place in the animals, in response to the various noxious stimuli being presented, were meticulously monitored. It was found that when the stimulus was presented, there was an immediate alarm

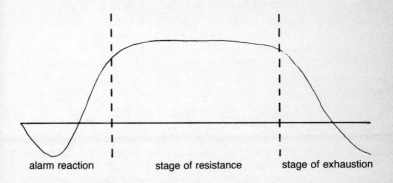

alarm reaction   stage of resistance   stage of exhaustion

Fig 1   General adaptation syndrome (reproduced from Selye, H, *Stress without Distress*, Fig 3, page 39 with permission from J. B. Lippincott Company).

reaction, in which all the physiological systems showed an increased level of activity to resist the danger. As long as the noxious stimulus was presented, this high level of physiological activity was maintained, even though the animal appeared to have adapted to the presence of the threat. After some time, at this high level of activity, signs of sickness began to be apparent, and damage in cells, tissues and organs was found. If the noxious stimulus persisted, and the high level of physiological activity was sustained, the adaptive energy of the animal appeared to run out. Exhaustion and death ensued.

This pattern of *alarm reaction, stage of resistance*, and *stage of exhaustion*, Selye called the *general adaptation syndrome*. Later investigations by myriads of other workers around the world showed that the pattern is the same in humans as in experimental animals. The mobilisation of the various physiological systems of the body to resist the noxious stimulus, Selye designated as *biological stress*. This is how he first defined it:

Stress is '. . . the state manifested by a specific syndrome which consists of all the non-specifically induced changes within a biologic system in response to a stimulus.'

Hans Selye, *The Stress of Life*, 1956

The meaning of this is not immediately clear to all readers, and many of my students have difficulty in grasping it, so let me try to elucidate. A syndrome is a group of symptoms which, together, point to particular change, or disease, in the body. The 'biologic system' is you or me. It is the 'non-specifically induced changes' that puzzle a little.

Non-Specifically Induced Changes

If someone sticks a pin in the back of your hand, or stamps on it with a heavy boot, there will be, in each case, differing changes in the 'biologic system' specific to the stimulus. But also, in each case, there will be the same 'non-specifically induced' changes of muscle tension, heart rate, blood pressure, breathing and so on, in response to the stimulus. These 'non-specifically induced' changes in your body, in response to any kind of stimulus, constitute biological stress. Later, Selye rid his definition of the jargon and simplified it, so that:

'Stress is the non-specific response of the body to any demand'.
Hans Selye, *Stress in Health and Disease*, 1976

It is on this concept of stress that all the lessons of stress management are based. If you want to manage your own stress, grasp this concept firmly. Internalise it, and make it part of your own thinking. That done, you are already well on your way to successful stress management, for now you know what it is that you want to manage. Since Selye published his first paper on the subject in 1936, over a hundred thousand scientific papers on clinical and experimental studies have been published in scientific journals in many countries and in diverse languages. Although different outcomes from similar studies are still frequently found, and the literature is littered with disagreements and contrary opinions, it would be an imprudent person who would argue, in the face of the evidence, that stress is an unimportant concept in the health of individuals, of families, of organisations and of nations.

You will have noticed that the definition on which this book is based emphasises that stress is your body's response to *any* demand. This means that we respond with stress arousal not only to noxious or threatening stimuli, but also to pleasant, welcomed stimuli that bring delight. Without stress, there would be no delight.

Stress is an essential part of the living process. We need stress just as we need food and water. Without stress in our lives, we do not grow properly – physically, mentally or socially. Usually, when there are not enough stimuli in our lives to provoke the physiological arousal that is stress, we are bored, so we go looking for stressful stimuli: boys chase girls, girls chase boys; some climb mountains, sail boats, play games, or join clubs, associations and political parties.

If our job is not adequately stressful, we soon become bored with it, and seek more excitement outside our occupation. If we are unemployed, or retired from a stimulating occupation, we have to find something to do to produce adequate stress arousal, or there is grave danger of chronic depression taking over. Involuntary unemployment, or even the threat of it, can produce chronic stress in the individual, which often leads to physical or mental illness, or both.

MANAGING STRESS

We need stress, but when we experience too much stress over a period of time, changes begin to take place in the cells, tissues and organs of the body, and various physical and psychological disturbances become apparent. The principles of managing your stress are really quite simple, but many people still need help to grasp these principles, and to apply them in their lifestyles.

In the course of a normal day, you experience many fluctuations in your stress arousal level. Such fluctuations in our daily lives don't do us any harm – indeed, they probably do us a lot of good. The real danger in stress begins when we live and work in circumstances where the stress level stays high for long periods, and does not get much chance to come back down near to base level (a low level of physiological activity throughout your body). Vast numbers of people lead lifestyles which have just this effect,

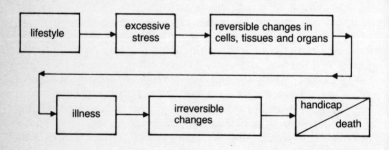

Fig 2   Consequences of stressful lifestyle.

and retribution, in the form of physical and/or psychological disturbance, will inevitably follow, as shown in Fig 2.

Fortunately, it is relatively simple to intervene at any of the first four phases, and to return to good health. Beyond the fourth phase, intervention may be difficult or impossible, and what life remains is likely to be severely handicapped. The fifth and sixth phases will require medical attention, and possibly surgical intervention. Many a coronary bypass might have been avoided, and many an ulcerated digestive system might have been saved through a change of lifestyle.

THE PRIMARY INSTINCT

The stress response is part of the primary instinct of all living things – the instinct of self-preservation. The *excessive* stress response is a learned response to stimuli, beyond what is necessary for self-preservation. Any behaviour that can be learned can also be unlearned. Stress management is concerned, not with getting rid of stress that is essential to our survival, but with learning to control and manage the level of the physiological response we make to any stimulus. Selye coined a new word, *stressor*, to describe any kind of stimulus to which we respond with the physiological arousal that is stress. So learning to manage stress means learning to manage our physiological arousal in response to the unending stressors we encounter in our daily lives. This is the psychomotor skill of stress management. In Lesson 1, we begin learning this skill.

Lesson 1: Basic practice position
1.   Lie down on the floor, or if that is too hard, on a settee or a bed, your legs stretched out and slightly apart. If your head is uncomfortable, put a pillow under your neck. If your back is uncomfortable, bend your knees.
2.   Let your arms lie alongside your body, your hands a few inches from your body, and palms turned down. Alternatively, rest your hands (apart) on your abdomen, elbows on the floor.
3.   Close your eyes.
4.   Pay attention to your own breathing cycle. Note how, as you breathe in, there is a slight rise of the chest and abdomen. As you

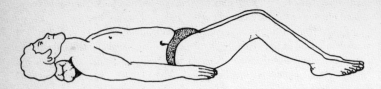

Fig 3   Basic practice position – lying.

breathe out, there is a slight fall of the chest and abdomen. Get used to recognising this rhythm of your own breathing, noting that it is not constant, but changes quite often.

5.   Now breathe out just a little more deeply, without forcing, so relaxing a little more the muscles of respiration, between the ribs, and in the abdomen.

6.   As you breathe out a little more deeply, let all your weight sag down on to the floor, or whatever you are lying on.

7.   Notice how, as you are lying there paying attention to the rhythm of your own breathing, there is a gradual quietening down of excitement in the nervous system, and a feeling of tranquillity. Practise this regularly for ten to fifteen minutes twice a day for a week. If you are so stressed that you think you cannot spare the time, then do it when you wake up, or just before you go to sleep at night. If you can practise again some time during the day, progress will be quicker. Once you have grasped the principle, you can practise this quietening down lesson sitting in a chair, in a bus, train or aircraft, or in a car – as long as you are not doing the driving.

Don't imagine that you manage stress by simply lying down on the floor. This is the beginning of the learning process, and forms the basis of the lessons that follow.

2
Understanding Stressors

That you have persisted as far as this, indicates that you have accepted Hans Selye's concept of stress or, at least, tentatively accepted it to see where the argument leads. If stress is all these physiological changes taking place within you in response to a stimulus, it follows that all the stimuli (or forces, if you prefer) that you encounter cannot also be stress. It was to avoid this likely confusion that Selye coined the word *stressor*, to describe the vast number of stimuli you meet every day of your life, which have the potential for causing you to respond with stress. Some stressors may be momentary and fleeting, provoking the arousal that is excitement or pleasure. Others may persist for days, weeks, months, and you may respond with a chronic high level of stress, always ready for fight or flight, bringing about the changes in cells, tissues and organs which become apparent in one physical illness or another, or the changes in behaviour which indicate a shift in psychological equilibrium.

Stressors may be encountered within ourselves, or in the external environment. Internal stressors may be such things as pain, sickness, memories, ideas, guilt feelings, thwarted ambitions, or poor self-concept. External stressors may be such things as heat, cold, noise, traffic lights, nuclear bombs, or any other kind of inanimate stimulus. They may be living things, like barking dogs, spiders, snakes or insects. But the vast majority of stressors we encounter are people, and it is certainly in the realm of interpersonal relationships that we are most likely to be provoked. As they say in Yorkshire, 'There's nowt so queer as folk'.

Stressors are not just stimuli that we meet intermittently. Just as we breathe air all the time, so we are encountering stimuli of one kind or another every moment of our waking lives, and frequently when we sleep, too, in our dreams. We meet them through every one of our senses, seeing, hearing, smelling, tasting and touching, and if any sense is defective, we may experience even more stress. To some stressors we do not respond at all; to some, we respond

19

with only slight stress. To others, we respond with a high level of stress, which may be brief or may continue for a long period of time. It is the cumulative effect of all our stress responses that begins to take its toll in illness and inefficiency. Fig 4 summarises a few of the stressors that we commonly meet with in our jobs and in our personal lives. The stressors act on us, and we react to the stressors.

These lists are by no means exhaustive, so you will probably have no difficulty in contributing your own additional stressors to each column. Let's look a little more closely at some of the stressors. You may not be in an occupation, so we'll start with the personal stressors first.

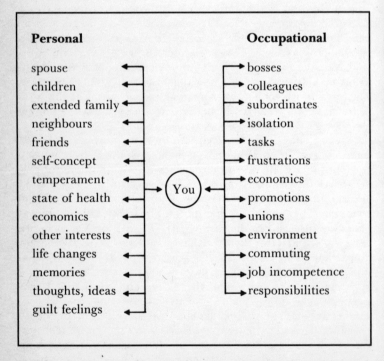

Fig 4   Common stressors.

HAPPY FAMILIES

It is a fact of life that those who are nearest and dearest to us tend also to be our most persistent stressors. Despite the efforts of the poets, the songwriters, the romantic novelists, and the almost universal desire to enter into matrimony, the relationships between husband and wife, and between parents and children constitute the most fertile seed-bed of stress. The family is the most important unit for the development of deep and loving relationships, but it is equally true that if you are going to be battered, physically or verbally, or mortally harmed, it is much more likely to take place in the comfort of your own home than in the dark back streets of a strange city.

As we grow up, most of us, consciously or unconsciously, develop a protective façade which we think enables other people to see us only as we want them to see us, hiding the reality of our weaknesses. Within the family relationship, such defensive façades are useless, and are brusquely swept aside by spouse and children or by parents. Spouses say and do things to one another that they would never dream of saying or doing another person, and these are not always in loving terms. Even in the most loving relationship, the veil is frequently torn away, and weaknesses exposed or threatened. If this happens frequently, the level of stress may be persistently high, and may become unbearable, a source of physical or mental illness, and a seed-bed for aggression and hatred, to replace love.

Handicap or illness in a wife or husband, or in a child, may be a stressor for the spouse or parents. The problems of looking after aged parents can also be a major stressor within the extended family. Events concerning strangers may cause a mild reaction in us; the same events within our family can bring a great deal of persisting stress.

LIFE CHANGES

During the 1960s, two American investigators, Thomas Holmes and Richard Rahe, examined the ways in which various common life events affected the health of individuals. They produced the

Social Readjustment Rating Scale (SRRS) of events which seemed to influence most strongly the health of the thousands of subjects interviewed. Each event in the 43-item scale was accorded a stress value, ranging from 100 points for the death of a spouse to 12 for Christmas and 11 for minor violations of the law.

Studies in the SRRS have been conducted amongst subjects in many different cultures. Although some of the items may not be applicable in all cultures, the general principle that a large number of changes in common life events is likely to lead to illness in the individual, is found to be true no matter where the study is conducted. When you consider how the pace of living throughout the world has been changing, how individuals and families have become much more mobile in terms of dwelling, income and social status, occupational stability, cultural changes, and family cohesion, it is not difficult to accept that such changes become stressors that handicap, maim and destroy.

Of the 43 items in the SRRS, 24 of them relate directly to intra-family relationships, and practically all the others relate indirectly to such relationships. Of the first 15 high-scoring items, 11 of them relate directly to relationships within the family, and the other four items strongly influence the family stability. Whilst the SRRS may not be currently making the same impact on social science research that it did twenty years ago, the data obtained from the many studies it initiated give a well-delineated picture of the family as a potential source of stress as well as love. We shall look at this more closely in a later chapter.

THE ENEMY WITHIN

If you look back at Fig 4, you will see that most of the stressors mentioned are things that lie outside ourselves. In technical terms, they are *exogenous* stressors, stimuli in our external environment, to which we respond with the physiological arousal that is stress. But stressors are not always 'those things or those persons out there'. Stressors are within ourselves, too – memories, thoughts, ideas, pain, guilt feelings, and ambitions, may all be stimuli to which we react with stress arousal. These *endogenous* stressors may at times be much more powerful in eliciting stress than anything outside, and may often be much more difficult to adapt to, without good professional help. Three of the items I have put in the personal column, self-concept, temperament and state of health, cannot really be classified as direct stressors, but I have included these because they are extremely important factors influencing the way we react to stressors at any given moment.

If you have a weak self-concept, it is more likely that you will be encountering activating stressors at every turn; if you have an exaggerated self-concept, you might well be creating stress in those with whom you interact, to your own disadvantage. With a sound self-concept, you will know something of your own strengths and your own weaknesses, and adapt more readily to the stressors you encounter.

Your temperament – that is, the kind of person you are now, the cumulative effect of all your life experiences and your reactions to these experiences – will also influence the way in which you react to a stressor, with joy or with fear, with tolerance or with aggression, managing or failing to manage your stress. I should emphasise that it is not so much the experiences you have had in life, but rather, the ways in which you have progressively reacted to those experiences (stimuli, stressors) that have turned you into the kind of person that you are now. Fig 5 shows only a few of these stimuli. Even if some of these items are inapplicable to you, their absence may be equally, or even more influential in your formation.

Two American psychologists, Friess and Woolf, sorted out five basic types of people, based on their reaction to stimuli. These ranged from the *hypoactive*, the passive, vegetable-like type who hardly ever seem to react to anything through the *calm, moderately active* and *active*, to the *hyperactive*, those who are easily triggered off to react violently to stimuli, to 'go up the wall' when crossed, and to become emotional about practically every issue. Despite the difficulties of assessment (we tend to see ourselves in the middle, and others at the extremes) and the fact that people can change if the stimulus is strong enough, this classification can sometimes be helpful. In their long-term studies into heart disease, Friedman and Rosenman designated a particular personality (Type A) to be a much more likely victim of heart attack than any other. Type A is the thrusting, driving, competitive personality, determined to succeed in every venture undertaken, 'engaged in a . . . chronic

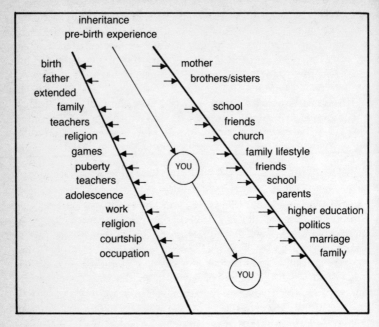

Fig 5 The rocky road to maturity.

struggle to obtain an unlimited number of poorly defined things from their environment in the shortest period of time and, if necessary, against the opposing efforts of other things and persons . . .'. Type A personalities are usually hard-working achievers, greatly in demand by employers, or successful in their own businesses, but they frequently have to pay a heavy price at an early age in terms of health.

Without limiting their achievements, or restricting their goals, it is quite possible for Type A personalities so to manage their stress that their health does not suffer in their unceasing quest for success. But it requires the will to do it!

STATE OF HEALTH

If you are feeling well, you probably won't react so violently to minor stressors. But if you have a headache, a nagging toothache, or painful indigestion, or if you are a woman in the pre-menstrual tension state, you may find that you over-react to minor stressors which at other times you might find amusing.

OCCUPATIONAL STRESSORS

Fig 4 also illustrates some of the stressors commonly encountered in our jobs. Stress at work is absolutely essential to retain interest and avoid boredom, but too much stress leads to inefficiency and absenteeism, with or without accompanying illness. For some people, work has no intrinsic value, and is seen only as a means of gaining money to carry on with real life. For others, work is real life, and anything that interferes with work – family, friends, holidays, sickness – is an irritation and an added stressor. Occupations are infinitely varied, and each may have its own specific stressors as well as those common to all jobs. Within any industry, school, university, coal-mine, hospital, office or department store there may be a multitude of stressors, but all workers do not respond to stressors in the same way. What is a stressor for one may be a joy for another.

Promotion and lack of promotion can be major stressors. Most people seek promotion, either for more money, or for improved status. I have known colleagues in higher education to become quite ill because of failing to gain the promotion which they thought their work deserved, and this happens in many industries. Others, competent at their work at a particular level, have gained promotion, only to find themselves unable to manage their reactions to the new stressors encountered, so that illness ensues.

Isolation at work is often a cause of increased stress. Social support is probably the most important external factor in managing stress. When we are unable to share with others the problems and difficulties we encounter at work, it is likely that our own chronic stress level will be relatively high. Suicide is the ultimate answer to all our stressors, and the idea is often toyed with by many.

At any given moment, asleep or awake, you are open to many stressors. In Fig 4 you are in the middle, and a number of stressors are present, from the personal side and from the occupational side. To some you react with physiological arousal, to others not at all. Your level of stress at any moment is the sum of the ways in which you are reacting to a variety of stressors.

THE UNCERTAINTY PRINCIPLE

Not knowing what to do in a given situation is one of the major evocators of stress, and is a common experience for us all. If a stressor is present, and you know how to handle it, there is likely to be only a slight physiological arousal, probably enjoyable. As the degree of uncertainty progresses, the stress level increases, as you explore or summon up more of your resources to adapt. It can be enjoyable; it can be exciting; it can be overwhelming. Once you learn how to manage your stress, you can remain calm in situations of uncertainty, and your ability to handle ambiguities greatly improves.

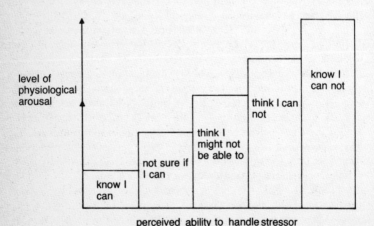

Fig 6   Uncertainty and stress levels.

Lesson 2: Relaxing the muscles of your face

Tension in face muscles is a very common consequence of stress reaction. This can lead to frequent headaches, facial pain, neck pain, bruxism (grinding your teeth, and even wearing them down). In this lesson, we concentrate on learning to relax the various groups of face muscles.

1.   Lie down in the basic practice position or sit comfortably in a chair.

2.   Run through Lesson 1, with which you should now be very familiar.

3.   *Jaw muscles*   With your eyes closed, press your teeth together rather firmly. Notice how your jaw muscles become tight and hard. If you can't feel this directly through the 'muscle sense', spread your fingers across each jaw, from the corner of your mouth to the lobe of each ear, pressing slightly against the face so that you feel the muscles tense. Now let the jaw muscles relax, and note the difference, through your fingers and through the 'muscle sense'. The 'T' (tension) signals have disappeared. In the course of your day, you have to use your jaw muscles a lot, in speaking and in eating – don't overwork them in response to stressors. Let your jaw muscles be relaxed when not engaged in eating or speaking.

4.   *Muscles of the forehead*   Frown heavily, exaggerating this beyond your usual style. Notice the 'T' signals from the muscles of the forehead above the nose as they tense up. Feel with your fingers if the 'T' signals are weak. Now let the muscles relax, the frown disappear, and notice the difference, through your fingers, and through the 'T' signals. Muscles of the forehead are connected over the scalp with other muscles at the back of your skull. Tension in one group leads to tension in the other, often producing headaches, a pain in the neck, or a feeling of tightness on the top of the head. When stressors are present, relax the forehead muscles instead of frowning, and tension headaches will not occur.

5.   *External eye muscles*   Close your eyes, and screw them up tightly in an exaggerated manner. You will probably notice how not only the eye muscles are tense, but there is tension all over your face, and possibly in other parts of your body as well. Now let your eye muscles relax, and notice the great difference as the 'T' signals disappear from the face and the body. Of course, it is very unlikely

that you walk around with your eyes screwed up as tightly as you made them a moment ago. But even when your external eye muscles are only slightly tensed, as happens in stress situations, there is a considerable arousal in the nervous system. Learn by practice to let your external eye muscles be relaxed, and so help other face muscles to be relaxed too.

6. *Muscles around the mouth* You can often recognise stress in other people by overt tensions in the muscles around the mouth. Maybe they press their lips together tightly, or bite their lip, or make odd movements of the mouth, or smile nervously, usually quite unconsciously. Such actions are a consquence of the stress arousal, and at the same time they send batteries of signals to the brain, producing more arousal in the nervous system. Make some of these movements yourself, noting the 'T' signals from the muscles, even in very slight movements of the lips and of the tongue, which is also an important muscle. Then let the muscles be completely relaxed, and note the difference. In stress situations, avoid such grimaces.

Many of my pupils, whose work has involved them reluctantly in public speaking, have found the relaxed face to be the key to success in making speeches which had previously been marred by dry throat, thick tongue, embarrassed stammering, or comical grimaces.

During the next week, try to become more conscious of these various tensions in your face muscles, during your daily practice. Observe other people's tensions, too. Apply your learning in potential stress situations at work or at home, letting all your face muscles be reasonably relaxed. Soon, this relaxation will become your automatic response to stressors.

3
The Unity of the Body

This book is meant to be not just a book about stress, but also a helpful guide to managing your own stress. The better you understand how stress can lead to happiness and growth, or lead to misery and decline, the more likely it is that you will persist with the practical lesson given in each chapter. In this chapter, and in the next, I want to look at how our bodies work, and just how excessive stress can lead to a variety of illnesses.

The division of the body into different systems is convenient for purposes of understanding and study, and in some cases, perhaps, for medical treatment. But it is a purely arbitrary division. What you are now, perhaps 70 kilos or more of complex tissues, organs and systems working more or less smoothly, highly skilful or lamentably clumsy, handsome or ugly, cultured or ignorant, has developed from a single microscopic cell. From your mother's ovum and your father's sperm, the zygote (as the newly-fertilised cell is known) has received the characteristics which will dominate and determine to a large extent its future development, and from somewhere it has received its built-in instructions to increase and multiply. So the one cell becomes many cells. The proliferating cells become tissues – nerve, muscle, cartilage, fat, bone. The tissues specialise into organs – brain, heart, liver, kidneys, lungs and so on, and the various systems develop. But the unity that was in the zygote still remains in your mature body, although the number of constantly changing cells has grown to countless billions, and each advance in scientific knowledge of the body has revealed more and more complexity of organisation. The development may be expressed as:

cell ⟶ cells ⟶ tissues ⟶ organs ⟶ systems ⟶ you

If all the cells in all the systems are in perfect condition, then you are in perfect health – possibly a rare condition in animals, including humans. If some cells in a tissue are not functioning properly, the tissue is handicapped, the organ to which it belongs is working below its optimum capacity, and the system to which the organ belongs is crippled in some way. This is probably the condition in which most of us live most of the time, when, in response to friendly enquiries about our health, we answer 'Very well, thank you!', and decide against mentioning the shortage of breath or slight stomach ache, the rather painful knee or occasional twinge in the lower back we have been experiencing lately.

When a large number of cells in any tissue become disordered or die, through injury, infection, what we eat or drink, or through the changes that take place as an outcome of chronic stress, then organs and the systems to which they belong are working at a great disadvantage, and you become ill, perhaps seriously. Any one system of the body working in a disorderly manner has an immediate effect on all other systems, the operation of some being slowed down, and of others speeded up. To a very great extent your body has its own built-in mechanism for repairing damage, fighting infection, restoring order where there is disorder. If you are sufficiently ill, you will go to your doctor, who will treat you according to the diagnosis he makes of the cells, tissues or organs which are mainly affected. In some cases drugs, to alter the functions of the cells and systems, may be prescribed. In others, surgery may be regarded as essential to repair or restore order. Or, possibly, you may be advised to modify your habits, change diet, give up smoking, go easy on the alcohol, take more exercise or more rest.

NO CURE FOR STRESS

Where the disorder in the body (call it illness if you prefer) is the result of excessive stress – the non-specific response of the body to any demand – there is no drug or medical treatment that can make any difference as long as you persist in responding to stressors with excessive arousal. Only a change in the way you manage your stress will have lasting results.

THE SYSTEMS OF THE BODY

The Skeletal System

This is often thought of as merely the convenient peg on which the important parts of the body hang, but it has many other functions. It contains the factories in which the red and white blood cells are manufactured, and it acts as a storage centre for calcium, essential in many bodily functions. In chronic stress, when physiological arousal never gets a chance to get back to normal, the factory and storage functions of the bones may become disordered, with distressing consequences for other organs and systems.

The Muscular System

The function of this system may seem obvious, but it is, in fact, much more complicated than is apparent. Not only do muscles move our bones at the joints, but they also form the heart, and pump the blood around the body, ensure a regular supply of oxygen to the lungs, play an important part in controlling blood pressure, and are essential to the utilisation of food in the alimentary canal. With our muscles we work and play, laugh and cry, acquire skills, achieve our ends. In acute stress, the muscles are instantly involved, and in chronic stress, constantly involved.

The *only* purpose of all the stress phenomena, other than in disease or injury, is *to enable muscles to contract effectively* in order to achieve some end, defensive or aggressive, creative or destructive.

The muscular system is the only system of our body over which we can exert direct control. If we do not contract muscle, we cannot move. If we do not contract muscle in the presence of a potential stressor, then we do not experience stress. It is through the muscular system, and *only* through the muscular system, that we manage our stress. As I will show later, we also think with our muscles.

The Cardio-Vascular System

This consists of the heart and the thousands of miles of blood vessels which carry food and oxygen to every one of the billions of

31

cells that make up the living body, and carry away the waste products for disposal. It includes also the blood, a front line of defence against invasion by harmful organisms. Its complex composition must remain stable in order to maintain health. The lymphatic vessels and glands, which act as the scavenging and recovery services of the body, and which produce the antibodies to fight against infections, are also important parts of this system.

Any stress episode produces great changes in the cardio-vascular system – increased heart rate, raised blood-pressure, tension in the involuntary muscles of the arteries, and many others, affecting the heart, the brain, the liver, the kidneys, the lungs, the digestive and lymphatic systems. Chronic stress produces changes in the cardio-vascular system which may lead to high blood-pressure (known as 'essential hypertension' before the stress factor was discovered, because its origin was unknown), coronary artery disease, hardening of the arteries, or stroke. Any changes in this system directly influence all other systems of the body for better or for worse.

The Respiratory System

This is the means whereby oxygen is efficiently extracted from the air around us, and supplied to the cells. At the same time, this system removes waste products, particularly carbon dioxide, and passes these into the atomosphere. The main organs which must be efficiently maintained are the nose and throat, the windpipe, the lungs and the muscles of respiration. Acute or chronic stress may produce changes which restrict breathing and influence oxygen uptake and waste disposal, to the detriment of other systems. These changes may have an important part to play in voice production in public speaking, singing or acting.

The Digestive System

Once described as a 32-foot tube with an appetite at one end, this is the system whereby we extract from chemical compounds in the earth the various chemicals that the body needs to function. It starts with good teeth, and its efficient working depends on a well-conditioned gullet, stomach, small and large intestines, assisted by the liver and some strategically placed glands. Acute stress has an immediate effect on appetite and digestive function. Chronic stress may lead to loss of appetite, irregular eating, gastric and duodenal ulcers, constipation or diarrhoea, or even ulcerative colitis. Any such changes may have a devastating effect on other bodily systems.

The Excretory System

This is the means used in the body to get rid of the waste products of the multitudes of chemical reactions going on all the time. The organs concerned are the kidneys and bladder, the end part of the alimentary canal and the skin, as well as the lungs, already mentioned. Stress has an immediate effect on the function of all these tissues and organs, and eventually on their structure, too. Any lack of efficiency in one of these organs is likely to have serious repercussions elsewhere.

The Reproductive System

Consisting in the female of the ovaries, the fallopian tubes, womb and vagina and mammary glands, and in the male of the testes and penis, this system has a direct two-way relationship with the nervous system and the endocrine system. Acute stress can immediately inhibit sexual desire or performance; chronic stress can lead to menstrual irregularity or frigidity in women, and to impotence in men. It may be a major factor in infertility, and is often a primal cause of frustration in marital relationships.

The Endocrine System

This consists of a number of glands in various parts of the body. They secrete chemicals called hormones directly into the bloodstream. Hormones are carried around in the blood, and interact with cells and organs and other hormones in a way which still presents many mysteries and occupies a large body of research workers around the world.

Lesson 3: Relaxing the hands and arms

After the face, tensions in hands and arms are the most commonly observed overt signs of stress in the individual. The researches of the neurophysiologists have shown that brain areas of sensory and motor cells relating to the hand are out of all proportion to the size of the hand. This we might expect, when we consider how skilful human hands become; the sensitivity they develop to a wide range of variation in touch, heat, cold, and pain; and the way in which they are so frequently used to communicate with others, whether in the anger of the clenched fist or the loving caress of mother and child or of sweethearts. In the hands, as well as in the face, we see the reflections of human joy and human grief. Through them we exhibit our love and our hate, perform the skills that keep us alive, and build a civilised society. In the stress reaction, hands and arms may be incessantly on the move – twiddling with pencils or other objects, clenching and unclenching, twisting a handkerchief, biting nails (a mixture of jaw and hand tension), wringing hands, finger tapping and so on.

When it occurs, this hand tension actually increases stress by alerting the brain centres and influencing the other bodily systems. It only serves to make you feel worse. Most of the muscles concerned with movements of the fingers and hands actually lie along the front and back of the forearm, so it is here that you must observe the 'T' signals and eliminate tension.

1.   Clench your fist, as tightly as you can. Notice how the muscles in the palm of your hand, and all the muscles in the front and back of the forearm become tense – and it is likely, too, that you will feel the tension spread up the arm to the shoulder, to affect the face and neck, and maybe even the abdomen. Now slowly unroll your fingers, and you will feel the restful wave of relaxation sweep over the other parts of the body which had tensed up with your hand.
2.   Your clenched fist was rather exaggerated, in order to make clear what really happens when you tense your hands. Try it once more, this time barely touching the tips of your fingers against the palm of your hand, trying to recognise the smallest amount of tension. Then let go, so that your hands and arms are completely relaxed.
3.   Experiment a little, pressing your hand against the floor if you

are lying down, or against the chair or table if you are sitting, learning to recognise instantly how your hand and arm muscles tense up, even slightly. It is not possible for muscles to tense up, even a little, without an instant increase in heart rate and blood pressure, with proportional changes in all other bodily systems. Relax these muscles, and the reverse changes take place in all systems. *This is how you manage your stress.*

4.   Once you have learned how the relaxed hand and arm feel, you must carry over this relaxation into your daily living. If your hands are not engaged in a purposeful task, let them relax. If you are standing, and your hands are unoccupied, lightly join (not clench) your hands in front of your body. In the presence of a stressor, relax your hands and arms, and relax the muscles of your face. It is difficult to be anxious or worried, angry or afraid when the hands and face are relaxed, because by purposely letting go the instinctive muscle tension you have short-circuited the arousal that is stress.

4
Living on your Nerves

The nervous system is the means through which you become aware of what is happening around and within you, and through which you act, consciously or unconsciously, to adapt yourself, by modifying the working of the various physiological systems. Nature has so evolved the nervous system that it keeps beavering away at the task of adapting you to your environment without you being aware of what is happening, or needing to think about it. This is the involuntary, or *autonomic* functioning of the nervous system. In this way the beating of your heart is modified, your temperature remains relatively stable, the rate of your breathing is varied, food passed into the mouth is fully utilised once it is swallowed, and a multitude of other essential functions go on in your body while you turn your mind freely to making money, making love, making other people happy or miserable, philosophising on the instability of human philosophy, or to the other important issues or trivia which occupy your life.

At other times the *voluntary* function of the nervous system is exercised. You will certain things to happen, and from the brain a message is sent through the nerve fibres to make muscles contract or relax to move parts of the body, or to stop them if they are moving. Such movements are not always made in response to your will. If you suddenly perceive a missile flying in your direction, it is likely that you will instantly raise your hands to protect your head, or duck to avoid the object before you have realised it is a danger. This is a reflex protective action. Unfortunately, it can also become an habitual way of responding to people and to life's situations. In such circumstances, it can lead to chronic stress.

VOLUNTARY AND AUTONOMIC SYSTEMS

The voluntary and autonomic systems are not independent of one another. If anything goes wrong with the autonomic system, it is likely that the voluntary movements will be affected. Whenever you contract or relax muscles, the autonomic system will adjust accordingly. When you take a walk, your muscles go into action, and all the other physiological systems spring into modified action to keep the internal milieu steady. You decide to hurry; the limbs move faster as muscles contract more strongly and more frequently through the voluntary system. Immediately, the heart beats faster, the breathing rate increases, more red blood corpuscles are pumped into the circulation, sweat glands open up to control temperature, digestion slows down, and many other internal changes are taking place through the autonomic system.

Sympathetic and Parasympathetic

The autonomic nervous system has two parts – the sympathetic system and the parasympathetic system, each with its own nerve fibres running from the brain to all the organs of the body. Their functions are reciprocal. In exercise, or in the face of perceived danger, it is the sympathetic which mobilises all the body's resources, that is, produces the stress response. When the danger has passed, the parasympathetic begins to work harder, bringing the organs back to normal, whilst the sympathetic influence is damped right down.

THE BRAIN AND COMMON SENSES

We have already seen that stress is the non-specific response of the body to any demand. It is an adaptive response. Most of our activities are adaptive responses to stimuli, whether we are wriggling our bottoms on uncomfortable seats, designing a new rocket to reach outer space, or merely wincing in response to a twinge of toothache. The nervous system controls this adaptation.

The brain is the central powerhouse and the control centre of the nervous system. To it there come messages from sense organs in every part of your body, keeping it informed of what is happening outside and inside the body. In the light of past experience stored in the memory, the brain interprets the meaning of the signals coming in, and, in response, sends signals to organs, muscles and glands to initiate the action necessary to adapt.

Some sense organs, or *receptors*, are specially constructed to receive information about what is happening at a distance from the body; the eye, the ear, and the nose are familiar as distance receptors, concerned with seeing, hearing and smelling. Other familiar senses are those of taste and touch. The taste buds on the tongue are the receptors for the former sense, but the latter, touch, has several different receptors. These distinguish light and heavy pressure on the skin, as well as heat, cold and pain, and are to be found in enormous numbers all over the surface of the body. Less familiar are the internal receptors, which pick up information about what is happening inside your body, and convey this information to your brain. Usually, you are unaware of the existence of these internal receptors until something goes wrong, and maybe you feel a pain in your inside.

Stress and Good Sense

The functions of these senses, and the way in which the brain interprets the signals being sent to it are important to our ability to adapt successfully. They are also important in understanding and managing our stress. The usual pattern of adaptation is as shown in Fig 7.

Using the visual sense as our example, the retina cells are stimulated by light waves (*reception*); signals are sent to the part of the brain concerned with sight (*cognition*); reverberations of electrical activity are sent around the brain, searching through stores of past experience to find the meaning of these signals (*interpretation*); having

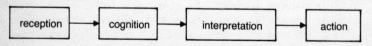

Fig 7   Usual pattern of adaptation.

found them, signals are sent (or not sent, if no action is necessary) to muscles, organs, and glands to take action to adapt. The first three of these steps constitute *perception*.

If the eye, the ear, or the nose, is not functioning properly, then the signal sent to the brain may be a false signal. The brain then has to interpret the meaning of this error, and makes a wrong interpretation. So our perception is false, and because of this maladaptive signals are sent to the muscles, organs and glands. This erroneous perception is a major cause of excessive stress in many people.

The Hypothalamus

The hypothalamus (Fig 8) is a relatively small part of the brain, but its groups of cells seem to be of enormous importance, particularly in connection with our emotional behaviour, and with stress arousal. It is directly connected with the various sensory regions of the cortex, and so is kept informed about what stimuli are being received in these parts. From the hypothalamus some nerve fibres run to important centres concerned with blood circulation and

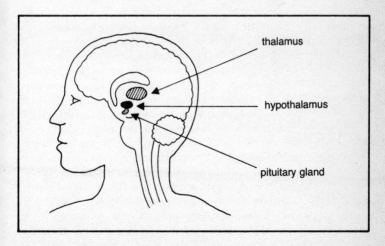

thalamus

hypothalamus

pituitary gland

Fig 8   The hypothalamus and pituitary gland.

breathing, while others directly influence the autonomic tracts and the endocrine system, to produce the non-specific changes that are defined as stress. The hypothalamus is the main anatomical link between mental and bodily functions, so that you may suddenly blush at your own thoughts, or experience stress when you think of the bills that remain unpaid, important tasks that remain undone, difficult encounters to be made in the future, or a narrow escape you have just experienced.

In Fig 7, the hypothalamus did not enter into the sequence of adaptation. If, however, the brain interprets the incoming stimuli (through any sense) as being threatening, the adaptive pattern is very different:

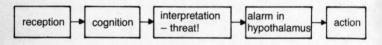

Fig 9   Adaptive pattern in perceived danger.

From the cerebral cortex, where the stimulus (stressor) has been interpreted as threatening, signals are sent directly to the hypothalamus to alert the defence mechanisms, and instantly a host of changes take place in your body.

From the motor area of the brain, signals are sent to muscles to contract, ready to fight or to flee – as many muscles, and as much tension, as the situation seems to require. At the same time, from the hypothalamus, urgent signals are sent through the sympathetic nervous system to all other systems to bolster up the muscles in their state of readiness. So the heart beats faster and more strongly; more red blood cells are pumped into the circulating blood from the spleen in order to supply more oxygen to the muscles; breathing becomes quicker and more shallow for the same reason. Blood-pressure is raised; temperature rises as this activity increases; more sugar is released from the liver to supply the necessary energy to the muscles. Tiny blood-vessels contract to shut off much of the blood supply to the digestive system and direct it to the active muscles; the muscular walls of the gullet, stomach, intestines, uterus, and bladder may go into spasm, producing the nauseating feeling of 'butterflies in the tummy'. In excessive reaction, which is not so uncommon, there may be involuntary vomiting, urination or defecation. Also, at the same time, instant signals are sent from the hypothalamus to endocrine glands to release hormones necessary for action, and to inhibit hormones which are unnecessary at this perceived defensive moment. This is the pattern of stress.

THE PATTERN OF STRESS

Note that in the stress pattern described, the action of adaptation to the stressor is through the contraction of muscle fibres. The instant arousal or damping down of the various systems takes place to ensure that the muscles have adequate fuel and adequate oxygen available for action, and a scavenging system alerted to remove promptly the waste products of muscular contraction. The increased output of *adrenaline* and *noradrenaline* serves to maintain the systems at a high level of activity, so that they continue to enable the muscles to contract until the emergency is over. Other hormones being produced in greater quantities help to produce the energy that the muscles need, and to repair the damage that is being done by this demand for muscular work. You enter into battle, or you run away (literally or figuratively) with all systems at 'go', hugely enjoying the excitement of this arousal, or just plain frightened by the stressor. The stimulus provoking this reaction may not be, in reality, a threat, and your perception may be false. But if you have interpreted it as a threat, the whole stress sequence unrolls, sometimes mildly, often excessively. This complex involvement of all the systems to enable muscular contraction to take place efficiently is the essence of adaptation if you do fight, or if you do run away. But, if you neither fight nor run away, then the whole response is, in fact, maladaptive and damaging to yourself.

THE KINAESTHETIC SENSE

We have seen that the purpose of all the non-specific changes that constitute stress is to facilitate and sustain muscular contraction for action. The level of stress is in direct ratio to the level of muscle tension in the body. If your muscles are slightly contracted, there is slight stress; if they are moderately contracted, there is moderate stress. If they are excessively contracted, there is excessive stress. This is true whether the stress is invoked by exercise or by the presence of a stressor. If the state of muscular tension is chronic, that is, going on for a long time, you experience chronic stress, and changes begin to take place in the muscles and in the other organs, systems and glands involved.

Fortunately, we have been endowed with the capacity to control the level of tension in muscles through the *kinaesthetic* sense, the 'muscle sense' previously mentioned. The kinaesthetic sense is possibly the most important of all the bodily senses yet, oddly enough, it is a sense about which most people have never heard. The word *kinaesthesis* comes from two Greek words, *kinein*, meaning to move, and *aisthesis*, meaning feeling. So the word is concerned with the feeling, or perception of movement of parts of the body.

The receptor organs of the kinaesthetic sense are to be found within the muscle fibres, in the tendons of muscles where they are joined on to the bones, and liberally spattered around the deep tissues which envelop all the joints of the body. These send messages to the brain to indicate variations in tension in the muscle fibres, and the changes within the joint as any kind of movement takes place. The late Dr Arthur Steinhaus, an eminent physiologist and Dean of George Williams University, a pioneer in stress management and a good friend from whom I learned many things, referred to these messages from the muscles as the 'T' signals, indicating the level of tension in the muscle. This 'T' signal I have happily borrowed for use in my own teaching. Kept informed by these ceaseless signals, we are able to execute, with greater or lesser accuracy, predetermined movements, for we always know the relative positions of different parts of the body. Through these sense organs, too, we can come to know the difference in a muscle when it is tense and when it is relaxed. Get to know your 'T' signals.

Developing the Kinaesthetic Sense

Usually, very fortunately, this sense works below the level of consciousness, the muscles tensing and relaxing to perform their task as demands are made on them, without you being aware of what is happening. To perfect a skill, like playing the violin, driving a car, putting a golf ball, or dissecting cranial tissues in an operation, you have to raise to conscious level the varying degrees of muscle tension and action required. Once successfully learned, accurate performance requires constant repetition, but also requires that the awareness of kinaesthetic function drops below the level of consciousness. If your skill level drops, you must come back to the basic practices.

So it is with the function of the kinaesthetic sense in the management of stress. If the level of stress is in direct ratio to the degree of muscle tension in your body, you lower the level of stress by relaxing muscles in the presence of a stressor. Learning to relax muscles requires a sharpening of the kinaesthetic sense, so that you learn to recognise easily when muscle groups are tensed. Once you know what the feeling of tension is like in specific muscle groups, you can consciously let the tension go, and so short-circuit the stress cycle.

It is easy to write 'you can consciously let the tension go', and very easy to read right past it without the significance sinking in. This I do not want to happen, for the fact that you can consciously contract and relax muscles is of the greatest significance in managing your own stress, although seldom appreciated even by those who do it most frequently and most expertly. Of all the different systems that make up the unity of your body, the only one over which you can exercise conscious control is the muscle system. Through it you can excite or quieten the nervous system; strengthen or weaken the cardio-vascular system; improve or damage the respiratory system, and modify for better or for worse all other systems and organs.

Lesson 4: Relaxing shoulder and upper back muscles
1.   Lie down in the basic practice position or sit comfortably, feet apart and hands resting on thighs.
2.   Run through the first three lessons, which you have now

43

practised well with some success, relaxing the relevant groups of muscles.

3.   Press your hands hard against the sides of your thighs. Apart from the tension you have already come to recognise in your hands and arms, note how the pectoral muscles, running from the front of your chest to just below the front of your shoulder, become tight and hard (Fig 10). Pay attention to the 'T' signals. If these are not clear enough, feel the muscle with your fingers, then check on the 'T' signals again. Let the tension go, and note the difference.

4.   Repeat the previous step, but this time note the tension at the back of the shoulder, tension in the muscles that run from shoulder blade to the top of your upper arm (Fig 11). Note the 'T' signals from the muscles. Let the tension go, and note the difference.

5.   Pull your shoulders up towards your head – an exaggerated shrug. Note the tension in the muscles running from the shoulder blades to the base of the skull and top of your spine, and from the point of your shoulder also to the base of the skull (Fig 11). Let these muscles relax, the shoulders drop, and note the 'T' signals disappear. Now shrug your shoulders only slightly. Note the tension you make in the muscles, then let the muscles relax, so that

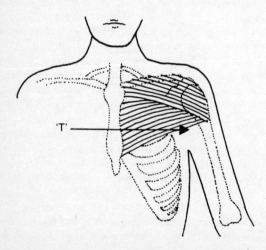

Fig 10   Pectoral muscles, showing tension point.

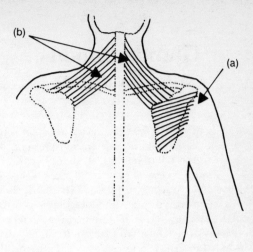

Fig 11 (a) Tension point in the muscles of the shoulder and upper arm; (b) tension points in the muscles of the neck and shoulder.

your shoulders drop. Almost invariably, in stress situations, these muscles contract and the shoulders rise. So avoid this, by letting your shoulders drop when you encounter a stressor.

6. As you lie or sit there, pull your shoulders back, in an exaggerated military manner. Note the tension in the muscles which run between the spine and the shoulder blades, and also between the shoulder blades and the top of your upper arm. Become aware of the 'T' signals. Let these muscles relax, and note the difference.

For the next week, practise frequently, in all kinds of situations, letting the muscles of your face, your hands and arms, shoulders and chest and upper back be relaxed, consciously. Try it, particularly, in potential stress-provoking situations.

5
Glands, Moods and Tempers

As we have seen, the purpose of the nervous system is to enable us to recognise what is happening in our environment, and to take action to adapt to these happenings, so that life can go on. As we are subject to stimuli, external or internal, every second of the day and night, and some form of response is required, the burden on the nervous system would indeed be formidable if it had to carry out every single adaptation. In fact, many of the necessary adjustments in the body's internal affairs are carried out by the endocrine glands, through the varied hormones secreted into the bloodstream in minute quantities, and carried to all parts of the body to influence the function of cells, tissues, organs and systems, and even other hormones. Some of the endocrine glands are shown in Fig 12. Others, not shown, include the ovaries in the female, and the testes in the male. These glands and their hormones play an essential role in the mobilisation process that is stress. Over-production or underproduction of any specific hormone, because of the way in which it interacts with other hormones, and through them controls and regulates the various bodily processes, may have a critical effect on our physical and mental health.

Stress arousal is a major factor in altering the production of hormones, and when it is a question of chronic stress, the imbalance may produce changes in physical, psychological and social health that are impervious to any kind of medical treatment. As this book is about stress management rather than about hormones, my comments will be restricted to some of the ways in which these two interact.

Earlier we saw how various physiological mechanisms are activated through the hypothalamus when a stressor is perceived as a threat. In Fig 12, for simplicity, emphasis is placed only on the suprarenal glands, because of the large number of hormones these produce. The pituitary gland is also of vital importance, however,

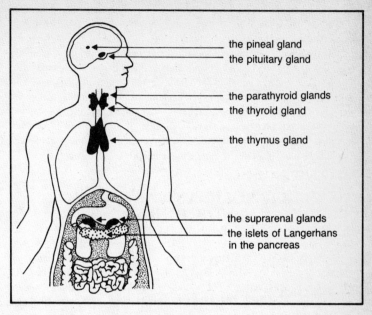

Fig 12   Location of major endocrine glands.

as it has a controlling influence on all the other glands.

The suprarenal glands lie, rather like admirals' cocked hats, on top of the kidneys. Each is actually two glands – the outer husk, known as the *cortex* (like the outer husk of the brain), and the inner core, known as the *medulla*. From the medulla two hormones are released, adrenaline and noradrenaline (known in the United States, where adrenaline is a trade name, as epinephrine and norepinephrine). A major function of these two hormones is to maintain at a high level the physiological changes brought about instantly through the sympathetic nerve fibres. Depending upon the amount of these hormones being released into the bloodstream, you can experience the feelings of stress arousal long after the stressor has gone. Until the excess is used up, you cannot get back to the baseline of low physiological activity.

As the hypothalamus triggers off the release of adrenaline in the suprarenal medulla, it is also activating the pituitary gland to influence the cortex of the suprarenal gland to produce a number of hormones known collectively as *corticoids*, but having many different functions. These hormones play an important part in spreading and sustaining the stress arousal, in breaking down some cells and tissues to provide energy for action, in activating repair and replacement mechanisms, and in conserving body fluids and salts. Many decades ago, Selye described these hormones of the cortex of the suprarenal glands as 'the hormones of adaptation'. As they diminish, the body's ability to adapt diminishes, too, and illness ensues. If they are exhausted, death is likely to follow.

CATABOLIC AND ANABOLIC HORMONES

Metabolism is the name given to all the processes that go on within the living body. A healthy metabolism is a balance of *catabolic* processes (breaking down stored fats, sugars and proteins to provide available energy for action), and *anabolic* processes (the building up of energy stores, the production of new cells, and the repair of wear and tear and damage).

Some hormones are primarily concerned with the breaking down process, and may be referred to as the catabolic hormones. During a stress arousal phase, these are to be found in the bloodstream in greatly increased quantities. Other hormones are primarily concerned with the building up and repair processes, and are referred to as anabolic hormones. During stress, their production decreases, so that the building up of energy stores, the production of new cells, the maintenance of the immune system, and the repair of normal wear and tear, or of wounds, cuts, scratches, and ulcers is slowed down.

In an important paper published in *Social Science and Medicine*, in 1981, entitled 'Biological Basis of Stress-Related Mortality', Sterling and Eyer, of the University of Pennsylvania, outlined the differences in metabolic activity during the catabolic and anabolic states of the body. Another way of referring to these states would be the *tension state* when, amongst other activities, muscles are contracted, and the *relaxation state*, when muscles are relaxed. Sterling

Catabolic State (tension)	Anabolic State (relaxation)
Halt in synthesis of protein, fat and carbohydrate	Increased synthesis of protein, fat and carbohydrate (i.e. growth and energy storage)
Increased breakdown of protein, fat and carbohydrates (for energy mobilisation)	Decreased breakdown of protein, fat and carbohydrates
Elevated blood levels of glucose, free fatty acids, low density lipoproteins, cholesterol	Less glucose, free fatty acids, cholesterol, etc.
Increased production of red blood cells and of liver enzymes for energy	
Decreased repair and replacement of bone	Increased bone repair and growth
Decreased production of cells for immune system (thymus shrinks, circulating white cells decrease)	Increased production of cells for immune system (white blood cells of thymus and bone marrow)
Decreased repair and replacement of cells with normally high turnover (gut, skin, etc.)	Increased repair and replacement of cells with normally high turnover (gut, skin, etc.)
Increased blood-pressure	Lowered blood-pressure
Increased cardiac output	Lowered cardiac output
Increased salt and water retention	Decreased salt and water retention
Decreased sexual processes	Normal sexual processes (cellular, hormonal, psychological)

Fig 13 Functional differences in metabolic states.

and Eyer's table is reproduced in Fig 13, with slight modifications.

From this you can see that any stress (response of the body to any demand) means an elevated catabolic state, and increased activity of the sympathetic nervous system. This is good for you, provided that the catabolic state is not sustained at a high level too long.

On the other hand, if you do stay in the catabolic state too long, the parasympathetic system does not get much chance to exercise its quietening influence, and the repair hormones are just not available for your protection.

The joy of living lies in striking a reasonable balance of change between the catabolic (tension) state and the anabolic (relaxation) state. Without being aware of it, vast numbers of people do this very successfully. Many others never seem to get the balance within tolerable fluctuations, and suffer accordingly. The more consistently the balance tips towards the anabolic state, so life may become more dull and boring – and fattening. As it tips towards the catabolic state, life becomes more adventurous, more challenging, more exciting, and also more likely to develop stress-linked health problems.

Weight Changes

As the catabolic (tension) state requires a high level of energy production, fatty tissues and protein tissues are broken down to supply this energy, and over time, the individual becomes thinner. This is often compensated for by over-eating as an antidote to stress, and weight is added.

High Blood Pressure

The increased output of adrenaline and noradrenaline, and of various corticoids serves to increase the volume of blood, the quantities of red blood corpuscles, the level of cholesterol, the tension in blood vessels, and the rate of heart beat. The likelihood of damage to the tissues and organs involved thus increases, possibly leading to kidney disease, hardening of the arteries and coronary artery blockage.

Infectious Disease

In the catabolic state, the thymus gland and the lymphatic system, essential to the mechanisms that protect against infection, shrink and become less effective in fighting invading micro-organisms. At the same time, the production of the white blood cells that protect against infectious organisms decreases, so that, if you 'pick up a bug', it is likely to take longer to get rid of it if the stress state persists. There is increasing evidence that allergies such as hay fever and asthma, and even cancer, may be adversely influenced by stress episodes.

Peptic Ulcers

Because the mucous membranes which line the alimentary canal are amongst those which have a high rate of turnover, the reduced production of repair hormones during the catabolic state may lead to a failure of the healing process when injury is caused to membranes during the process of digestion and excretion. Gastric and duodenal ulcers, and ulcerative colitis are examples of failure of the healing process, and are common outcomes of excessive stress.

Skin Troubles

Skin cells are also replaced frequently, and their replacement may be retarded by faltering mechanisms of repair and replacement during chronic stress periods. Psoriasis, urticaria (nettle rash), and acne may not always originate through stress, but there is adequate evidence that the healing process is inhibited to a greater or lesser extent by increased stress. The healing of skin wounds, cuts, and grazes is retarded during stress episodes. You can rub on as many ointments as you can find, but if the cause of the persistent skin trouble is stress, only a change in behaviour will bring about the healing.

Sexual Behaviour

Many hormones are directly related to sexual function. Over-production or underproduction may strongly influence sexual behaviour and inclination, and the functioning of the sex organs. It is on this knowledge that the various contraceptive pills have been developed. We have already seen that during stress episodes there is an increase in catabolic hormones, and a decrease in anabolic hormones. All of the known sexual hormones are anabolic hormones. So, in acute or chronic stress states, there tends to be a loss of interest in sex, and a diminution in the sex drive. This happens to men and women, being perhaps slightly more common amongst women. Within the family situation, this loss of interest in sex by one of the partners may lead to disturbed relationships, and increased stress within the family.

The fluctuation in the production of sex hormones accounts for the pre-menstrual tension syndrome which occurs in many, but by no means all women. The changes in hormone output leading up to the menstrual period, perhaps affecting the hypothalamus, the pituitary gland, the ovaries, the uterus and the cortex of the suprarenal glands, may produce many of the overt signs of the stress syndrome – irritability, muscular tension, aggression, clumsiness and other symptoms. Because this syndrome is apparent only in some women, and may vary greatly in expression amongst this limited number, the existence of a pre-menstrual tension syndrome has been frequently rejected. In recent years, its existence has been recognised in law, being successfully used as a defence plea in cases of women being tried for criminal behaviour.

It is possible that fluctuations in hormonal output as a result of excessive stress in males may also be a factor in some criminal behaviour. It may also be a root cause of accidents. Scientific evidence for this is not yet available, but it is common human experience that we are most likely to have an 'accident', injure our backs, or be aggressive towards others when we are in a bad mood or a flaming temper.

Rheumatic Diseases

Over a million people in the United Kingdom, and over five million in the United States suffer from some form of rheumatic disease. It is more prevalent amongst women than amongst men, and is described in the textbooks as 'a disease of unknown cause'; there is no known cure, either.

A few years ago, two nurses working in a rheumatology clinic for out-patients in a Sussex hospital came to see me. They wanted to attend a workshop I was organising at the Royal Society of Medicine in London, on behavioural medicine, stress management, and the management of rheumatic diseases, led by Dr Robert E. Rinehart, an American rheumatologist. The nurses were distressed that year after year, the same patients continued to attend the clinic for treatment, but whatever treatment was offered, very few patients showed signs of improvement. Some became more ill from the iatrogenic effects of the drugs prescribed. In the event, the nurses did attend, but only four rheumatologists attended the workshop, with many others who had been invited indicating, in effect, that '. . . neither I, nor any other rheumatologists I know, have any interest in stress management as a form of therapy in rheumatic diseases.'

Many years before, Dr Rinehart was an orthodox rheumatologist, an Associate Clinical Professor at the Oregon University of Health Sciences, the son of a distinguished rheumatologist, and the third generation of physicians in his family. He had begun to lose faith, in the early fifties, in the various approaches he was using in the treatment of his patients, with very little success. Aspirin, gold salts, heat treatment, the much-vaunted corticosteroid drugs, physical therapy – all seemed to have beneficial effects for a short time, but very little permanent effect. Some of the hormone drugs being used effectively alleviated rheumatic pain, but in time produced serious side-effects through disturbance of hormonal balance with, in some cases, fatal effects.

During the fifties, Rinehart had worked for brief periods with Selye at McGill University in Montreal, and had seriously considered the implications of stress theory applied in his own speciality, rheumatology. About the same time, through the influence of Dr Henry H. Dixon and Dr Herman A. Dickel, two Professors of

Psychiatry at Oregon University of Health Sciences, Rinehart encountered the work of Dr Edmund Jacobson, a distinguished psychophysiologist whose clinical and experimental studies on the maladaptive effects of chronic muscular tension were arousing great interest in many fields, and popularising the concept of relaxation. Rinehart worked for some time with Jacobson in Chicago. On his return to Oregon, he trained some of his ancillary staff – nurses and physiotherapists – in Jacobson's approach to the control of muscular tension, and began to use this as his main form of treatment for patients suffering from various rheumatic diseases, with only a limited use of drugs for the alleviation of pain, or for potentially fatal immunologic complications. For the next thirty years, the results were spectacular.

Where patients learned to control their muscular tension, and used this skill in their everyday life, there was a gradual relief of pain, and a gradual disappearance of the rheumatic symptoms in thousands of cases. Where the orthodox treatments had been tried and failed, this new treatment, the diminution of the stress response through tension control, led to new lives for thousands of patients. In 1982 I met a number of his patients who told me their stories of how this new approach had changed their lives. The frequently stated opinion was not that something new was being done to them, but that they were at last learning how they could do something for themselves.

Mental Illness

Changing moods and tempers are accepted as being part and parcel of human expression, of reasonable or unreasonable adaptation to stimuli, within ill-defined limitations of swing, frequency, and time. When the degree of change, the number of changes, or the length of the period of change becomes excessive, we see the individual's behaviour as maladaptive. In vulgar terms 'there's something the matter with him', or 'he's off his head', or 'he's going round the bend'. The word neurosis has been coined to express any continual kind of behaviour that is maladaptive. To a very great extent, we are all neurotics at some time or another. Sometimes we need help to change our neurotic behaviour, and for this we may turn to the psychotherapist – perhaps a psychologist, perhaps a psychiatrist, the latter combining the functions of physician and psychologist.

The practices conducted by the two psychiatrists mentioned above, Drs Dixon and Dickel, were, during the 1930s, mainly concerned with the more severe cases of mental illness. Various schools of treatment, mainly psychoanalytic, were utilised to try to help patients. They reported, rather cynically, that 'the benefit given was proportional to the number of techniques that we had in those days', an approach that, in the present day is euphemistically termed eclectic psychotherapy. The term 'biological stress' had not yet entered the medical vocabulary, but both men knew of the syndrome under other names.

As a student at Northwestern University Medical School, in Chicago, Dickel suffered from chronic juvenile arthritis. He was advised by physicians that learning to relax might help him to handle the chronic problem of pain. With scepticism, he tried it and, to his surprise, he found, not only relief from pain, but an increased ability to live with arthritis. Dixon had worked for many years with Dr Steven Walter Ranson on defining the physiology of the hypothalamus, and together they had noticed some relationship of the hypothalamus to emotional disorders, and to chronic muscular tension. The full relationship of the hypothalamus with the sympathetic nervous system and the output of hormones as described earlier was yet to be discovered.

Apart from their patients with severe mental illness, Dixon and Dickel were often approached by outwardly healthy individuals suffering from anxiety and associated illnesses, but who could get little help from their physicians. Such patients were almost invariably exhibiting muscular tension, leading Dixon and Dickel to name the syndrome 'the anxiety tension state'. They began to introduce their patients to Jacobson's techniques of tension control, using a staff of skilled nurses who were initially trained in the teaching techniques. So successful was the outcome of this new learning, that it became the main form of treatment for all 'anxiety tension state' patients. In the next four decades, long before 'stress management' had become fashionable, some fifty thousand persons learned, through the Dixon and Dickel clinics, to improve their own health by tension control. Nevertheless, what they were learning was to manage their stress through controlling their own tensions, in exactly the same way as the lessons in this book can help you to manage your own stress.

BEHAVIOUR THERAPY

Following the Second World War, Dr Joseph Wolpe, a distinguished psychiatrist at Temple University, in Pennsylvania, was developing the field of applied science that was to become known as behaviour therapy. At a certain stage, Wolpe found that it was often helpful to teach neurotic patients who had difficulties in personal relationships to express themselves more openly to others. Assertiveness training became an important part of treatment, and a keystone therapy which is now widely used. But while assertiveness training was found to be useful in diminishing anxieties which arose from interpersonal relationships, Wolpe found it was of no value in diminishing anxiety which had its origin in areas other than interpersonal relationships, a finding which perplexed him for some time. In his seminal book, *The Practice of Behaviour Therapy*, Wolpe relates how he was inspired when he encountered the clinical and experimental work of Edmund Jacobson in helping individuals to reduce muscular tension, an inevitable concomitant of anxiety.

Once he had grasped the implications of muscular relaxation, Wolpe began to teach this skill as an essential part of his treatment of neurosis, and, in particular, the treatment of phobias. In doing this, he opened up a completely new field of psychotherapy, known as *systematic desensitisation*, that is widely used in all countries.

As Dixon and Dickel had found twenty years earlier, Wolpe found that the reduction of muscular tension through relaxation training is a vital tool in the treatment of many forms of mental illness. This approach is now shared by most psychotherapists throughout the world, but others, particularly general practitioners in medicine, continue to rely mainly on tranquillising drugs as the means of combating the various forms of anxiety in their patients.

Psychological imbalance is frequently an outcome of acute or chronic stress. Through muscular relaxation in the presence of the stimulus, the whole of the stress phenomenon is mitigated, the function of the sympathetic nervous system is short-circuited, the excessive production of catabolic hormones is inhibited, and the sense of threat and anxiety is diminished or not present at all. You can get help from a psychotherapist in learning this skill, or you can learn it from the lessons in this book.

Lesson 5: Relaxing the neck muscles

Many years of teaching experience convince me that the most stubborn tensions are to be found in the neck and just above the shoulder blades. Alleviation of tension here requires much time and patience, but the reasons for it are not hard to find. The neck is a very complex piece of architecture: a column of seven small, oddly-shaped bones, the cervical vertebrae, held together at more than a score of unstable joints by a dozen ligaments cunningly interwoven to withstand stress and strain, and yet allow great freedom of movement.

Between the vertebrae lie spongy pads of cartilage, *the interverte-bral discs*, which serve to cushion the spine and brain against shock, and to protect the nerves which run out from the spinal cord between the vertebrae. Degenerative changes occur in the discs, so that the nerves may be affected by pressure, to produce pathological changes and neck pain. These conditions require medical treatment, and medical advice should be sought before you assume that neck pain is due to muscle tension and stress.

1. Lie down in the basic practice position. Run through the first four lessons, relaxing the face muscles, hands and arms, chest and shoulders and upper back. After a few minutes, press your head backwards against the pillow, or other base. You will feel tension in the muscles at the back of your head and neck, and probably down your back as well. Hold it for a few seconds, so that you are really aware of the 'T' signals from the muscles, then let the muscles relax so that your head lies loosely on the pillow, with no tension at all in your neck muscles. After a few minutes, press your head back again, only slightly this time, trying to recognise the faintest 'T' signals from the muscles. As soon as you are aware of this tension, let it go, relaxing your neck muscles completely.
2. As you lie in the basic position, raise your head and neck slightly. You will feel the muscles at the sides and front of your neck becoming taut, and possibly the tension will extend down your

57

abdomen. Hold it for a few seconds, become aware of what the tension feels like – the 'T' signals – then let it go, relaxing these muscles so that the weight of your head falls down on the pillow. Check on tensions in these muscles during the day, whether sitting, standing, moving about, working, or lying down.

3. Don't lead with your chin. Check your habitual posture, making sure that your head rests centrally on top of the spinal column, neither with your chin poking forward too much, nor your head drawn back in a military posture. Either deviation means that the natural curve of your neck will be distorted by chronic muscular tension so that, in addition to the interference with the blood supply to your muscles, the mechanical relationships of the vertebrae are disturbed, with the possibility of added pain. Moreover, tension in the neck as a result of bad posture is a stressor in itself, and is likely to lead to increased tension in other parts of your back and arms.

4. Are you a shoulder-shrugger? In Lesson 4, I drew your attention to tension in the muscles of the upper back. These muscles are closely allied to the neck muscles which will also tense up when shoulders are raised. Many people go through life with their shoulders held higher than is necessary, placing a strain on muscles of the neck. Check yourself frequently to see if your shoulders are raised, even slightly. If your neck muscles are tense, let go. Soon this letting go, letting the shoulders drop, will become an automatic action.

Help improve the blood flow through the muscles of your neck by relaxing the muscles and *gently* rolling your head around on your neck in a wide circle, first one way, then the other. Do this frequently during the day for a few seconds, and you will find it relieves your neck wonderfully. By managing the tension in your muscles, you are also managing your stress.

6
Stress Management in the Individual

Any method of stress management can be deemed to be successful if, at the end of a specific learning period, the learner can honestly say that he is able to manage his stress more effectively, even if it is merely a placebo effect. People learn despite poor teachers, but learn more easily if the teacher is good, the method intellectually acceptable, and the pupil willing. Learning has been defined as being a change in behaviour as a result of experience. No change in behaviour simply means that nothing has been learned, whether this is due to bad methods, bad teaching, or a bad pupil.

INTERVENTIONS IN STRESS

In Fig 9, we noted the five phases in the adaptive pattern when a stimulus is encountered that is interpreted as threatening, evoking the stress arousal for action. To manage stress, intervention may be made at any one of these stages, as shown in Fig 14.

Avoiding Stressors

In the first phase, *reception*, avoidance of a stressor makes sense at times, but makes nonsense at other times, perhaps becoming neurotic and maladaptive. Wearing gloves when handling hot, cold or rough objects diminishes stress. Running to mummy may be an adequate response in a child seeking protection, but an adult constantly looking to others for protection is maladapted. Changing one's job may be the only solution to stress at work but frequent change of job to avoid stress almost certainly shows that the problem lies in the individual rather than the job. A happy, lifelong marriage is still the ideal for all cultures in the world, and divorce is next to bereavement in the Social Readjustment Rating Scale as life's most stressful experience. A second marriage has been

	Phase	Intervention	Initiator
1.	Reception	Avoid stressor; close eyes; shut ears; wear gloves; run to mummy; change jobs; get rid of difficult spouse; etc. etc.	Yourself (with or without the advice of a friend, physician or counsellor)
2.	Cognition	Drugs or alcohol	Yourself or physician
3.	Interpretation	Psychotherapy, drugs or alcohol	Yourself, physician, psychotherapist or counsellor
4.	Alarm and Stress Response	Drugs or alcohol	Yourself or physician
5.	Muscular contraction (for action)	Relax muscles; don't allow contraction to take place in the presence of potential stressor	Yourself (with or without the help of a teacher)

Fig 14   Interventions in stress.

described as '. . . a triumph of optimism over experience', but a second divorce is almost certainly a sign of maladaptation. Running away from stressors is only occasionally the right way to manage stress.

Alcohol and Drugs

At the second and third phases, *cognition* and *interpretation*, the brain cells become alerted by the incoming stimuli and work out their meaning. Mankind has from time immemorial found a solution to stress in alcohol and other drugs. Alcohol is often described as a stimulant, but it is, in fact, a depressant of the nervous system, making the electro-chemical transmission of signals from one nerve to another more difficult. It affects, first of all, the higher rational and judgemental areas of the brain, then, gradually, it dulls the ability of the brain to receive incoming messages, or to interpret their meaning accurately. After a few drinks, the party goes better, for even the more inhibited conversationalists find their tongues are loosened, and the talk becomes noisier and more trivial. So alcohol is sometimes a good thing.

On the other hand, it is a drug that affects not only the brain, but many other organs and tissues of the body, as will be attested by anyone who has experienced a hangover. As we drink more, our judgements about our own ability to judge become clouded, so that we imagine we are more clever, more wise, more skilful as inversely these qualities diminish in us. Some drivers think they can drive better with a few drinks, but their brains don't work quickly enough to receive and interpret incoming signals and to act on the interpretation, so that injury and death may result.

For thousands of years, mankind has found other substances from plants which have been helpful in clouding the nervous system, and so reducing anxiety and worry, two common aspects of stress. The result is the present day multibillion-pound traffic in illicit drugs. Hallucinogenic or narcotic drugs such as mescaline, opium, cocaine, heroin and many others seem to be in greater demand than at any time in history, so that drug dealers and their victims cheat, lie, steal, wound and kill to obtain them and to market them, usually in the most affluent societies in the world.

Pharmaceutical companies compete with one another to produce a bewildering array of new drugs that alter moods and feelings, and have many other effects not clearly understood. Few medical practitioners are hesitant about prescribing these to patients who complain of illnesses which have no apparent organic basis. Like alcohol, such drugs may be beneficial in small quantities until the patient learns to modify his own stress behaviour. Continued for a long time as a passive control of stress behaviour, they are more likely to produce dependence, loss of integrity, and other forms of illness.

The Mind-Menders

At the third phase, false *interpretation* of the meaning of the incoming stimulus as a threat may be the major cause of the stress arousal. This tendency is not always easy to overcome, certainly not by drugs nor by muscular relaxation alone, and it may require periods of psychotherapy. Different schools of psychotherapy abound. If you think you need this kind of help, make sure your chosen therapist is suitably qualified and trained.

The Beta-Blockers

At the fourth phase, the *alarm and stress response*, the hypothalamus sends its signals through the sympathetic nervous system to all other systems to start working overtime. A new approach to this response was developed in the late sixties and seventies. It temporarily raised the hopes of the medical profession for a big step forward in the treatment of stress-related illness, and, with vast sums being spent on publicity, the hopes of the international pharmaceutical companies for recouping their research investments with interest. This was the development of the so-called beta-blockers.

We saw earlier how, when a stimulus is interpreted as being threatening, the hypothalamus sends immediate and direct signals through nerve fibres to arouse the various organs to a higher level of activity for suitable adaptation. These electro-chemical signals enter the organs through special receptors on the organs, called beta-adrenoceptors, which then conduct the excitement to the whole organ to get on with the job. The function of the new drugs, developed not from plants, but through manipulation of molecules in chemical compounds, was to block the beta-receptors so that the electrochemical impulse in the sympathetic nerves could not cross over into the organ, thereby assuring that no arousal could occur, despite the presence of a stressor to which the patient usually responded. Unwanted stress was about to be eliminated.

Classic studies appeared on the effects of propranolol and oxprenolol (two of the most widely used beta-blockers) showing how they reduced heart rate in surgeons performing operations, diminished stress in musicians performing on stage, steadied the aim of rifle shooters in competition, controlled examination nerves in students, and turned hesitant public speakers into articulate orators. A very high-powered conference of distinguished physicians, psychiatrists and cardiologists, convened in 1980 by Ciba-Geigy Pharmaceuticals, a main producer of beta-blockers, was ecstatic in its praise of these drugs as a means of reducing stress and mitigating the effects of cardio-vascular disorders. There was no mention in the conference nor in the index of the adverse side-effects of these drugs, but with the passage of time, these have been found to be not inconsiderable. The prospect of reducing stress in industry by issuing all workers, from the chairman to the office boy and the cleaners, with a daily beta-blocker may yet loom on the horizon.

Tension Control

At the fifth and final phase of the adaptive sequence, muscles contract for the action – to fight the stressor or to run away from the stressor. This, after all, is the whole purpose of the stress response. The majority of stressors we encounter are interpersonal, and we cannot usually become aggressive nor run away. So we experience, in the presence of the stressor, all the feelings of stress arousal, but we must smile and say 'Yes, sir, no, sir' or whatever; the bodily systems have prepared for action but we do not act. This is maladaptive and, in the long run, injurious to health.

As we saw in Chapter 4, the only physiological system over which you have direct control is the muscular system. If, in the presence of the stressor, whatever it may be, you are able to control the tension in your muscles, you will, in direct ratio, manage the level of your stress, without the use of alcohol or drugs or any other aids. Reducing tension may not be a beta-blocker, but it certainly is a beta-cheater, as it restricts the amount of available noradrenaline necessary to trigger off the organs to become more active. The evidence for this, in the lives of millions of people, is so overwhelming that it is impossible to refute it. But because learning to relax muscle tissue in the presence of a stressor may take time and practice, the option is frequently rejected by physician and psychiatrist in favour of a pill which is more easily prescribed and administered.

SURVIVALS AND NEW ARRIVALS

As with types of drugs and schools of psychotherapy, there are numerous approaches to stress management through physical methods, and some metaphysical methods. Holding someone's hand, or giving them a cuddle, is a natural way to help reduce stress, but you can't go around cuddling strangers with impunity. Massage – even in the less salutary parlours – helps temporarily to reduce tension in muscles and to remove waste products from muscle tissues, but in the middle of a row, you can seldom take time out for a massage. Prayer can be of enormous help in reducing stress in those with faith, but when stress is present, even those with strong faith may find it difficult to pray.

More stylised approaches would include *autogenic training*, a system devised by a German psychiatrist, J.S. Schultz. After the Second World War, Schultz's students carried the system to other countries, the main protagonist being Wolfgang Luthe in Canada and the United States. In turn, Luthe's disciples carried it to other countries, but it was not until the seventies that autogenic training was imported commercially into England by Dr Malcolm Carruthers, of the Maudsley Hospital, in London.

Autogenic means 'beginning within myself', and the training is based upon Schultz's extensive studies in hypnosis as a form of therapy. The patients are taught to concentrate on a series of six different exercises:

1 and 2.   Self-suggestion of heaviness and warmth in the upper and lower limbs by, for example, saying inwardly 'My right arm is heavy; my right arm is heavy and warm', etc.
3.   Self-suggestion of regularity of heart beat.
4.   Self-suggestion of calm breathing.
5.   Warmth in the abdomen (said by Schultz to be based on the relaxing effects of a warm bath).
6.   Self-suggestion of coolness in the forehead.

Schultz found that many patients, with varying diseases, who were responding poorly to orthodox treatment, made remarkable recoveries when introduced to autogenic training. AT has always been regarded as a form of therapy, and its adherents insist that it be taught only under the supervision of a qualified physician because of the occasional catharsis experienced. If you like auto-genic training and you can afford the fees, there is a good chance it will help you manage your stress.

Meditation in its various forms claims to help you manage your stress, and there is no doubt that it may do so. Perhaps the best known variation is Transcendental Meditation, introduced into Europe and America by a Hindu mystic, Maharishi Mahesh Yogi, in the 1960s. Amongst the many temporary proponents were the pop group, the Beatles, whose every activity was regarded as newsworthy. When, in fashionable pursuit of the wisdom of the East, they dabbled in Transcendental Meditation in the full glare of the world's media, this produced world-wide publicity for the movement, which gained rapidly in adherents and wealth, and turned Maharishi Mahesh Yogi into the most famous yogi in history.

Other yoga disciplines, usually in a much emasculated form, are widely taught in Europe and America, and claim to help alleviate stress. Many classes, often composed of overweight matrons aspir-ing to the comely shape and lithe limbs of attractive teachers, are courses in simple exercises, including various *asanas* or postures, and simple breathing exercises, to which are attributed some marvellous but unsubstantiated physiological and therapeutic effects. Again, if you like yoga classes, they may well help you manage stress.

Stress arousal means increased heart rate, blood-pressure, tem-perature, and, amongst many changes already mentioned, increased ability of the skin to conduct electrical activity from inside the body outwards (the galvanic skin response, or GSR). Currently, instru-ments for measuring such changes, small enough to be held in the hand or to be wrapped around the finger, or carried in the pocket, are widely used on the recommendation of physician or psycho-therapist, and are freely available as aids in the management of stress. In Europe, Aleph One of Cambridge, is a major supplier. You may find that such an instrument will be useful to you.

Others find that exercise and sports help them work off the muscular tensions that have developed in a busy day or week, and risk the possibility of injury or other reaction that might arise simply because of the high level of stress induced by the exercise. If you favour exercise as a means of reducing your stress, just make sure you are fit enough to undertake the exercise.

PROGRESSIVE RELAXATION

The lessons contained in this book, to help you manage your own stress, are based on the clinical and experimental studies of Edmund Jacobson, a very remarkable psychophysiologist and physician, whose work has widely influenced many fields of physical and mental health, education and sport, work and play since early this century. I first encountered the works of Jacobson in about 1950, as a lecturer in physical education at the University of Otago, in New Zealand. His seminal book *Progressive Relaxation*, first published in 1929, showed, amongst many other things, how muscular tension diminishes skill performance and slows down skill learning, both areas of learning with which I was concerned at that time. This control of muscular tension was of considerable professional importance to my students, training to be teachers of physical education.

Managing stress can only be done through managing muscular tension. There is no other way. All the different approaches I have mentioned above, and the many others I have omitted, only achieve their end through reducing muscular tension. I was influenced by the logical and scientific basis of Jacobson's tension control to use it as a direct method of managing stress, and this is what I still teach. But I have to admit that not everyone finds this detached, scientific approach easy to follow, so many will opt for autogenic training, yoga, Transcendental Meditation, psychotherapy, or exercise, or just stick to prayer and hope for the best, or that the worst will never happen. If the chosen method proves successful, it is only because the final common pathway is through reduced muscular tension and progressive relaxation, as shown in Fig 15.

Lesson 6: Relaxing lower back and abdomen muscles
A large number of men and women over the age of thirty (and quite a large number much younger) in this country suffer from low back pain as a result of muscular tension, often a consequence of stress.

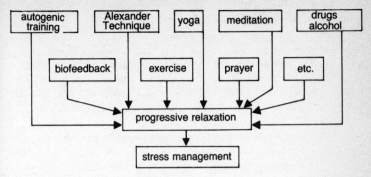

Fig 15   Pathways to stress management.

For some, it is just a dull, throbbing pain at the end of the day, accepted as a consequence of the day's labour. For others, it may be a sharp, stabbing pain, prompting visits to the doctor, and gaining them the status of 'lumbago sufferers'. It may also mean a slipped intervertebral disc, or a muscle torn as a result of effort. Many of these troubles develop from excessive muscular tension over a period of time, whether it be in household chores, factory work, sitting at a desk, or even lying in bed. They may be due to postural habits of standing, sitting, lying or moving. Such tensions arise and increase when you are experiencing stress, and you are much more likely to injure your back when you are angry, jealous, worried, anxious, tired or just plain fed up.

Check the tension first in the basic practice position. If you have a painful back, tackle this lesson with care!

1.   After you have been lying down for a few minutes and gone over the lessons you have already learned, arch your lower back strongly. Hold the position for a few moments, long enough for you to note the 'T' signals from the muscles of the lumbar region. Now relax these muscles, so that your spine drops back towards the floor.

2.   Now you must try to recognise the very slightest amount of tension in this region, arching your back only a little, then let the tension go immediately you sense it. Check on it also when you are lying on your side, for you may be one of those who lie all night with

67

your back arched, and so lay up a store of unnecessary backache and stress for yourself each day.

3.   Next, sit on a chair – an ordinary dining chair or desk chair is best – and let your hands rest on your thighs. After a few seconds, sit up as tall and as straight as you can – reach up with the top of your head! Hold this absurd posture for about twenty seconds, noticing how your back has become tense, from your seat to your head; how the weight of your body has shifted forwards towards the edge of the seat; and how the muscles in the front of your thighs have also tensed up. It is likely that you will feel generalised muscular tension throughout your body, increasing stress, the arousal of all the bodily systems. Now let your muscles relax, so that your spine curves, you become less tall, the weight of your body moves back to your buttocks, and your thigh muscles relax too. You will have reduced stress, and will now be sitting much more comfortably. You need never practise this exaggerated posture again, but, occasionally, just sit up straight, and note the tensions that are immediately apparent, then let them go.

4.   Once you have learned to recognise this tension in your back, you will find you can sit more comfortably anywhere. You will be able to stand more comfortably, too. The guardsman who stands to attention with the muscles of his back strongly tensed is much more likely to faint than his neighbour who stands well, but relaxes his back.

5.   Check on tension in abdominal muscles by pulling in the abdominal wall tightly, and noticing the 'T' signals from these muscles. Let the muscles relax. It is important to have good strong abdominal muscles, but it is not good to hold them tense for any period of time. In stress situations the abdominal wall tends to tighten up. Learn to relax these muscles.

7

Stress Management in the Organisation

Where two or three people are gathered together, the seeds of potential stress are being sown. The family, the workplace, and the team can all be bastions of self-fulfilment or self-realisation for the individual, or they can be the main vector for the accumulation of stress, and destruction of individual personality. Conversely, excessive stress in an individual within a family, an organisation, or a team can diminish its efficiency or lead to its destruction. Here, I will deal only briefly with two organisations, the family, and the school.

THE FAMILY

Whatever your personal viewpoint of family life, families are essential to the growth of integrity in the individual. Families, natural or adopted, are the soil in which people grow and learn to live. Like a plant, the child can grow well, physically, psychologically, socially and spiritually, if the soil is good, and can learn to handle stress. If the soil is poor, with constant strife between parents, or lacking a parent, or with distress or illness in a parent, the child may have to live with a great deal of insecurity and uncertainty before he has learned to handle it. Chronic stress may become a companion for life.

Love is the essential basis for managing stress within the family. Love is the essential nutrient element that will give the child a chance to grow in every way – it is far more important than good food or pretty clothes or material comfort or good education. A baby learns to love by being loved. If he does not learn to love within the family, it will be more difficult for him to give or to receive love in later years. This is a major and important factor in handling the stress of living. In an earlier chapter (*see* Fig 5), I pointed out that the kind of person you are now is not so much due to the experiences you have had, but rather to the way in which you have reacted to those experiences. This is equally true in the development of love. Just as surely as physical and mental traits are passed through genes from one generation to another, so love, the greatest of the virtues, is also passed on from one generation to another by example. If it is present in the parents, it is likely to be present also in their children but, unlike blue eyes and curly hair, a child can reject love.

Personality Development

Erik Erikson postulated a hierarchical development of nine senses on the way towards integrity of the adult personality. The basis is love in childhood. If the child is loved (and of this he can only be aware by the way he is fed, handled, watered, cleaned and cuddled) he learns to trust. *Trust* is developed in the first year of life, when the child learns that his world is relatively stable and rewarding. If, on the contrary, the world is more often unstable and unrewarding, the sense of trust develops not very well or not at all.

From the second to the fourth year of life, the sense of *autonomy* develops. The child becomes aware that he is a person in his own right, not just part of significant adults, and begins to assert his own will, his claim to possessions, his claim to be independent. This is the stage that brings out the 'oohs' and 'ahs' and proud admiration of parents and grandparents. But if the earlier sense of trust is poorly developed or independence is discouraged, the acquisition of the sense of autonomy may be restricted or delayed, and the seeds of future distress implanted.

From about three years to around seven or eight, the child is freely developing the senses of *initiative* and *imagination*, acquiring new skills and experiences, trying out new ventures, experiencing failure and trying again. If trust and autonomy are reasonably well established, they form a sound basis for new enterprises, and for coping with failure. If they are lacking, or poorly developed, it is possible that the child's initiative and imagination will be restricted, just at a time when the opportunities of play school or real school are beginning to offer. Frustration may be more difficult to handle.

From six or seven onwards, the child is acquiring the senses of *application* and *industry*, learning to begin a task, work at it, and bring it to completion. If the earlier senses have been insecurely established, the child may have some difficulty with application and industry, may become impatient with learning, easily distracted, and may begin to incur the displeasure of parents and teachers. New sources of future stress are being built into the developing personality.

Round about eleven years, and on until sixteen or seventeen, the crucially important sense of *identity* is emerging. From the significant adults around him, from the reactions of his peers, and from his intuitive awareness of his own successes and failures in mental, physical and social performance, the growing youngster begins to be much more aware of himself as a worthy or unworthy person, appreciated or not appreciated by others. If the earlier senses are reasonably well developed, it is likely that the teenager will develop a sound identity: a modest appreciation of being of value to himself and valued by others; an awareness of his or her masculinity or femininity; an ability to tolerate criticism and hostility.

If, somewhere along the developmental channel, the earlier senses have been frustrated, it will be that much harder to develop a positive identity. Encountered stimuli, instead of being interesting or exciting challenges, may be too readily perceived as threats, and the stress arousal, even when maladaptive, may become an habitual reaction.

The next sense to develop moves the growing individual out of the family sphere – the sense of *intimacy*. Its growth, too, depends on what has gone before. This sense of intimacy is not what the tabloid newspapers mean when they use the word in connection with some scandal. In Erikson's terms, it means being able to establish sound, friendly relationships with other persons, on a basis of mutual trust, equality, respect and liking. It is a developmental need of the teenage years, beginning around thirteen or fourteen with peers of the same sex. Boys may form their 'gangs' or privileged groups to pursue excitement together, from which others are excluded; girls form their own little groups, and have their shared goals, or secrets, or tasks. A great deal of learning goes on within the group – mental, physical, emotional, sexual, social and moral or immoral – and close friendships are formed, which may last a lifetime.

In later teen years, the emphasis in relationships shifts naturally to the opposite sex, seeking an intimacy that may not be immediately associated with fornication or marriage. If there has been difficulty in establishing a sound identity, the insecure child may have a lot of problems in relating with intimacy to other peers, for this intimacy also means revealing your true self to others, and this can be threatening. It may also lead to difficulty in relating intimately to the opposite sex, so that the real self is protected by a façade of outward show and deceit, leading to misunderstanding, later rejection and further stress.

Finally, in Erikson's hierarchy, comes the sense of *generativity*, a rather ungainly word, encompassing an interest in babies, a drive towards marriage and founding a family, together with the physical sexual drive. The successful acquisition of all these senses leads to the *integrity* of the individual personality and temperament, the ability to adapt to the stress of life, and to become the well-adapted, responsible parents of the next generation about to be born and to start going through the same process of growing up.

We know, of course, that it rarely happens in this ideal way. Over the years, the intimacy of parents may evaporate, infidelity corrupt, and poverty and illness frustrate, so that children may have to grow up making their way carefully through an unending minefield of stressors. Many of the mines they successfully dodge around; others explode and leave them emotionally scarred for life, always on the defensive, expecting other mines to explode around them, perhaps unable to relate readily to other people, or to relate lovingly or sexually to a potential mate. A genuinely loving relationship in later life may heal the early wounds, but not too easily. A psychotherapist may be an essential helper.

If one or other of the parents is experiencing excessive stress, whatever the reason may be, the pent-up physiological arousal may be vented on members of the family, with frequent verbal or physical batterings. The 'battered wife' syndrome and the 'battered baby' syndrome are almost certainly indicative of excessive stress in the one who batters.

Menopause

A critical period in family stress is during the menopause of the mother. This 'change of life', when the reproductive role of the woman is coming to an end, may last only a few months in some women and, in others, for several years. It may pass almost unnoticed, or it may provoke in some women quite marked changes in physical and mental health, due to the relatively large variations in hormonal output. With some women the sexual drive may be diminished, leading at times to disharmony and argument, and outbursts of bad temper. If the husband understands what is happening to his wife, he can be a great stabiliser in family relationships. Unfortunately, most often men do not understand what is happening to their wives in menopause, and they may respond with frustration and anger, creating more stress.

To compound the family difficulties at this stage, mothers in menopause (which can happen at any time between 40 and 50 years) may also have children in their teens, who are also under-going significant hormonal changes preparing them for their future roles as father or mother. These fluctuations in hormonal output in teenagers may sometimes be as disturbing as in the menopausal mother. If, as is very often the case, no one understands what is happening, much unnecessary conflict and stress can afflict the entire family.

STRESS IN SCHOOLS

Education is one of the major and most important industries in all countries. The workers in education – professors, lecturers, teachers, head teachers and ancillaries – are all industrial workers. The difference between their industry and coal-mining or automobile building or banking is that their product is not an inanimate object. It is the formation of a real, live, breathing, thinking and arguing person, and we have already seen that where two or more people are gathered together . . .

Teaching, whether in a school, in a university, or in a management training centre, is a variable task, even for the very best of teachers. On some days it is easy, pleasurable and satisfying. On other days, with the same subject and the same class, it is difficult, demanding, unpleasant and not satisfying at all. Teaching adults is usually more demanding intellectually than teaching children, but with the latter there are, for some teachers all of the time and for all teachers some of the time, almost insoluble problems of asserting and maintaining discipline, which frustrates the primary task of getting on with the teaching and the learning. Possibly, loss of discipline in a class is the major stressor in schools, creating stress not only in the teacher, but also in the children. Discipline, or order, if you prefer the word, is an essential condition of planned learning, and if it is not there, the task of the teacher is much more onerous and the education of the children in the class is restricted. Two or three poor teachers with disorderly classes in a school can, and often do, undermine the disciplinary ethos of the whole school, producing stress in other teachers, and throughout the organisation.

Teaching is very much an isolated occupation. For most of his professional life a teacher is isolated in a closed room with 20, 30 or even 40 children. He rarely sees another teacher teach, and within the profession, it is not done to comment on the incompetence of a colleague, even when one does observe him teaching badly. So the stress that builds up in the job often finds an outlet in opposing authority – head of department, head teacher, governors, local education authority or the Minister for Education and the government of the day – and sowing stress elsewhere.

The head teacher in a school is also in an isolated job. If he is competent and supportive of staff, there will be good order in the school and less stress, much of what there is being assimilated by the head, often with quite serious consequences for his mental and physical health. If the head teacher is experiencing excessive stress, whether from pressures of personal or occupational stressors, the consequences for other teachers, the children and the school can be disastrous (*see* Fig 16).

A school is a living, active organism. Sometimes it is strong and healthy; at other times weak and sickly and in need of overhaul. It has many external stressors and many internal stressors. Getting rid of external or internal stressors is rarely an easy task. As we have already seen, what is perceived as a stressor by some people in an organisation may be enjoyed by others. It may be wise and necessary to change some conditions or situations for the good of

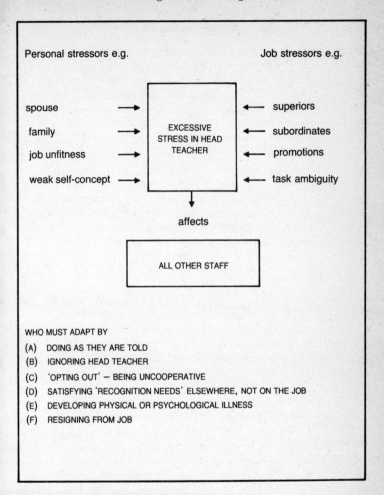

Fig 16 'Stress in Schools' model. (This may also apply in any other industry, substituting 'Manager' for 'Head Teacher'.)

all, but other conditions and situations are integral to the school and cannot be changed.

Children under Stress

Schools and teachers, as already observed in Fig 5, make a strong impact on the development of temperament over a period of many years, as well as providing the three Rs and other aspects of education. School is an essential stressor for all children. Some react to it happily, with excitement and enjoyment and thrive on the experience. Other children react with excessive stress. They may become ill as a result of their stress arousal, or develop habit patterns of stress in response to any kind of authority, which may last for a lifetime. The conflict between parental expectation and the child's ability may also be a continual source of stress.

There is a strong argument for including a fourth R in basic education – that is *relaxation*. This can be, and in a few schools is already, included in the physical education or health education programmes without additional time being required. Experience of this teaching in schools in Britain, America, Sweden and Denmark has shown that it can have a positive effect on pupils and teachers alike.

There is no absolute solution to stress in schools other than to abolish them altogether, transferring the stress elsewhere. But for each individual teacher there is a solution if he or she wishes it: learn to recognise stress in yourself. Learn to manage your own stress, that is your physiological arousal in response to stressors around you.

Lesson 7: Relaxing the muscles of legs and feet.

Like the muscles of the arms and hands, the muscles of the legs and feet play an important part in creating and publicising our stress. You have only to observe people sitting in a bus or train, or at a board or committee meeting. Frequently, when a poker face or joking word gives nothing away, the restlessness of the legs and feet may reveal a great deal. Feet tap impatiently on the floor; ankles bend and twist; knees are crossed over into incredibly tense positions, and frequently changed over; sometimes a foot is curled around the leg of the chair, or, when the knees are crossed, the foot is bent up and down and wiggled from one side to the other.

There are many leg muscle groups in which these tensions occur, so you have to find out for yourself which of these is a factor in your own stress response.

1. Start by sitting comfortably on a chair, your knees about six inches apart. Rest your palms on top of your thighs.
2. Now run through all the previous six lessons which you have already been practising, and let all these muscles relax.
3. Press your feet hard against the floor, pushing slightly forward. Notice how, under your hands, the muscles of the front of your thighs become tense and hard. Hold the position for a few seconds, then let the muscles relax. The 'T' signal ceases, as does the pressure of the feet on the floor. Repeat this with diminishing pressure on the floor, until you are able to recognise the faintest tension in the muscles, and to let it go.
4. Once again, press your feet into the floor, this time pulling backward against the resistance of the floor. Notice how the muscles of the back of your thigh become tense and tight (you may feel the additional pressure against the chair). Hold the position for a few seconds, aware of the 'T' signals, then let the muscles relax. This is the kind of tension you must learn to recognise – the muscular tension that is present even when there is no movement.
5. The twisting ankle, the tapping feet, the curling toes are all further indications of tension and stress. These are best checked in the sitting position, with one knee crossed over the other. As with all the other muscle groups, exaggerate the tension for some seconds, and note the 'T' signals from that area. Then let the tension go, so that the particular muscle group is now quite relaxed and floppy. Point your toes towards the floor, and note the tension in your calf muscles at the back of your leg. Bend your ankle, bringing your toes up towards your knee, and note the 'T' signals from the front of your leg. Turn the sole of your foot inwards, and note the feeling of tension in the front and inner side of your leg. Turn your sole outward, and note the tension in the outer side of your leg. Curl your toes under, and note the 'T' signals from the sole of the foot, and from the calf muscles. Habits of tension in these muscles can often be the cause of painful cramp. If you let the muscles relax, the tension goes, and the stress diminishes. Once you have learned to recognise the tension signals from your leg muscles, check frequently when lying, sitting, standing, or driving, so managing your own level of stress.

8
Measuring Stress

PERSONAL INVENTORIES

Numerous personal inventories (most relating to anxiety or mental health) to be completed by the individual have been developed in many countries, and are frequently used in clinical conditions. You can find these in any standard psychology textbook.

The inventory shown overleaf is the Psycho-Somatic-Tension-Relaxation Inventory (PSTRI). It was developed some years ago for use with my own students, and has proved useful. It relates to mental, physical and social aspects of health, all of which, according to numerous research papers, are likely to be influenced by your level of stress. Each of the items is a common state of health or form of behaviour or way we feel about ourselves. Some of them apply to everybody, without exception; a few may not apply to you at all.

Spend about ten minutes completing your answers, without spending too much time philosophising on any particular item. Do not mark the book. Jot down your ratings on a piece of paper, then add to find your total score.

EVALUATING YOUR SCORE

Used with many hundreds of men and women, the mean score on this test is 54, with a wide standard deviation of 22 points. There is no significant variation with age, nor between men and women. Compare your own score with the scores shown below, and you will have a reasonable knowledge of your own level of stress, provided you have recorded your scores honestly, and with some insight. You will also learn what you might do, if anything, to improve your score. Remember that all inventories are rough instruments, so that the interpretation assigned to scores cannot be exact, but they are useful guidelines to understanding your stress, and subsequently managing it.

PSTR Inventory

Consider each of the following statements *carefully*. Decide how it applies to you, then write down your rating for each statement, showing the frequency of the occurrence, according to the scale below

Frequency
Very often – 4
Often – 3
Sometimes – 2
Seldom – 1
Never – 0

	Item	Rating
1.	I suffer from backache	2
2.	My sleep is fitful and disturbed	1
3.	I have headaches	2
4.	My jaws ache	2
5.	I get upset if I have to wait	4
6.	I get pains in the back of my neck	2
7.	I am more nervous than most other people	4
8.	I find it hard to get off to sleep	1
9.	I feel a tightness or tingling in my scalp	1
10.	I have stomach trouble	1
11.	I lack confidence in myself	4
12.	I talk to myself	2
13.	I worry about financial problems	3
14.	I get embarrassed when meeting people	3
15.	I have fears that something dreadful is about to happen	2
16.	I get tired during the day	2
17.	I have a sore throat in the evening which is not from infection	2
18.	I am restless and cannot sit still	3
19.	My mouth gets very dry	3
20.	I have had heart trouble	0

21.	I feel I'm not much use	4
22.	I smoke	0
23.	I get 'butterflies in the tummy'	2
24.	I feel unhappy	2
25.	I perspire	4
26.	I drink alcohol	1
27.	I am self-conscious	4
28.	I feel I am going to pieces	3
29.	My eyes get tired and sore	2
30.	I get cramps in my legs or feet	2
31.	My heart pounds rapidly	3
32.	I am afraid of meeting people	4
33.	My hands and feet get cold	1
34.	I suffer from constipation	2
35.	I take various pills and medicines without doctor's advice	4
36.	I find myself in tears rather easily	3
37.	I suffer from indigestion	0
38.	I bite my nails	4
39.	I have a humming in my ears	1
40.	I have to empty my bladder frequently	3
41.	I have trouble with gastric ulcers	0
42.	I have skin troubles	1
43.	I get a tightness in my gullet	2
44.	I have trouble with duodenal ulcers	0
45.	I worry about my job	3
46.	I get ulcers in my mouth	0
47.	I worry about trivial things	4
48.	My breathing is shallow	2
49.	I get a feeling of tightness in my chest	2
50.	I find it hard to make decisions	4
	TOTAL	112

Interpreting Your Score

The scores shown here are each one half of one standard deviation, rising above or falling below the mean score of 54 points. If your own score comes between the figures shown, you will have to juggle a bit more with the suggested interpretation.

Score

98   A score at this level means that you are really damaging your own health by excessive stress reactions. You will almost certainly need some advice from a qualified psychotherapist, who can help you reduce your perception of stressors, and improve the quality of your life.

87   A score at this level indicates that you are experiencing too much stress, which is having a damaging effect on your health, and probably on your personal relationships. It is important that you learn to reduce your own stress reactions, for you are hurting yourself, and may also be hurting others by your behaviour. It will probably take a lot of time and practice to learn to control your stress, and you should seek professional help.

76   A score at this level would suggest that your level of stress is moderately high, and could begin to be harmful to your health. You should consider carefully how you react to stressors, and seek to reduce this physiological arousal by learning to control your own muscular tension in the presence of stressors. A good teacher will help you, or use a suitable audio-cassette.

65   With a score at this level, you probably get a fair amount of excitement and stress in your life. Occasionally, there will be periods when there is too much, but you probably have the capacity to enjoy the stress, and to come back down to a quieter level fairly quickly, so that there is not likely to be any threat to your health. Some relaxation would still be helpful.

54   With a score round about this level, it is likely that you are able to control your own stress reactions, and that you are a fairly relaxed person. Probably you respond to the various stressors you encounter without interpreting them as threatening, and so you are likely to have easy-going personal relationships and can tackle your work without fear or without loss of self-confidence.

43   A score at this level would suggest that you are not too easily aroused by the stressors you encounter, or maybe you are just indifferent to the things that go on around you. It is unlikely that your health will be affected negatively, but your enjoyment of adequate excitement may be limited.

32   A score at this level would suggest that you are probably leading a rather dull life, and seldom respond even to exciting and pleasurable events that occur. Perhaps you should take up more social or recreational activities to increase your stress arousal.

21   If you only managed to score around this level, it may mean that you don't experience enough stress in your life, or that you have not analysed yourself accurately. Maybe it would be a good idea to become more active, and to seek a little more excitement in work, social life, or recreational activities. Taking relaxation lessons would be futile, but some counselling might prove helpful.

If you have followed the instructions in the introduction, you will be rating yourself for the first time before starting to read the book. When you have completed the book, and practised the lessons over about eight or ten weeks, complete the PSTR Inventory again, to see if your stress quotient is changing.

If your score lies between 43 and 65, you are in a comfortable stress category, which does not call for changes in lifestyle. If your score lies below 43 or above 65, then it is likely that you need to modify your lifestyle, with some more excitement at the lower level, and better stress management at the higher level.

9
Quietening the Restless Mind

Since psychologists entered into the stress arena some three decades ago, they have become – apart from health educators – the most dominant profession therein, particularly on the research and theoretical aspects. Because of the tendencies of academic psychologists to seek innovation, they have often also tended to become like the medieval philosophers alleged to be in continuous wrangle about the number of angels who could dance on the head of a pin, bringing learned obscurity to what has been eminently clear to common sense and common experience.

Frequently rejecting Selye's original definition of stress, which forms the basis of this book, many have used the term *psychological stress* in diagnosing the needs of their patients. Search as I will, I can find no definition of psychological stress, even in the papers and volumes dedicated to its examination. Indeed, I believe that it is merely another Humpty-Dumpty term, meaning what the author wants it to mean, sometimes more, sometimes less. Uncertainty, indecision, mental conflict, and mental depression may all be psychological symptoms of acute or chronic stress, but to describe these by themselves as psychological stress is an abuse of words. Nor can the emotional states of anger, fear, jealousy, or hatred, be described as psychological stress, as emotions are non-existent without the physiological changes that are biological stress.

We have already seen that many people suffering from stress-related illnesses, mental or physical, can be greatly helped by psychotherapy, learning to perceive differently such potential stressors as spiders, snakes, husbands, air travel, job failure and a million others. If it is successful, patients learn to reduce their stress reactions and to return to whatever normality may be. This may produce the hoary fallacy that 'it's all in the mind'. But psychotherapists can be, and often are, wrong. Even the renowned Sigmund Freud has turned out to be a bit of a fraud.

BODY AND MIND

Somewhere in his Satires, Juvenal wrote

'Orandum est ut sit
Mens sana in corpore sano.'

It is to be prayed that there may be a healthy mind in a healthy body. We say amen to that, but there is often confusion about what is of the body, and what is of the mind. When teaching stress management techniques through control or management of muscle tension, I am often told 'Oh, I can relax my body all right, but it's my mind that keeps tense. I can't relax my mental activity at all, and my mind keeps going on and on.'

There are two important points here. First, there is no such thing as mental tension. Whatever the mind may be, it is an abstract entity, over which philosophers have pondered for thousands of years, and it cannot become physically tense like muscle tissue. Secondly, whatever the mind may do, it cannot do it without some form of muscular contraction. Usually, the term mental tension is meant to convey the idea of mental conflict, an inability to resolve a problem or many problems, or the frequent, almost overwhelming recurrence of one idea after another, so that clear thinking becomes difficult. Accompanying these occurrences, there will invariably be muscular tensions in various parts of the body, particularly in the eyes and throat, and other physiological changes that are stress. When the ideas flashing through your mind are associated in any way with a threat to your welfare – economic, social, physical, loss of love and so on – it is likely that the tensions will be very much greater, the level of stress will be enhanced and, in turn, will contribute further to the sense of insecurity. It can be very tiring, too!

MENTAL AND PHYSICAL REST

Many years of clinical experience and experimental studies have shown beyond dispute that it is possible for most people to learn to quieten down the mind by learning to relax the muscles of the body. When the ability to do this is learned, one can then snatch short periods of complete mental and physical rest, leading to a diminution of the stress level, even in the course of a very busy day. As pressure of events mounts, and personal stress grows, a short period of complete relaxation lasting only a few minutes can do as much good as an hour's sleep, and help to restore confidence and clear thinking in an astonishing way.

Contrary to common belief, there is abundant evidence that thinking is not only an affair of the mind, but is intimately associated with muscular contractions as well. You cannot think unless you use your muscles. Edmund Jacobson showed this experimentally more than half a century ago, and his work has since been verified by other scientists. You have only to think of a few everyday experiences to see how thought and muscular activity are intimately connected. The demagogue, in his efforts to convey his thoughts to his audience, bangs the rostrum or waves his arms to add heat to the coolness of words; the sports enthusiast will use his body to convey his thoughts more clearly, and the more excited he is about the game, the more muscular activity will be involved; and the agitated or angry (that is, in increased state of stress) man or woman will frequently convey their mental excitement by exaggerated facial gestures, restless eyes, and louder than usual voice. Such behaviour is common with the extrovert individual, and usually he finds it easy to communicate with others for he is using his mental and physical resources together.

VERBALISERS AND VISUALISERS

All thinking is a combination of activity in the brain and action of the speech muscles and the eye muscles, that is, *verbalisation* and *visualisation*. We are all both verbalisers and visualisers, but not to the same degree. Some are predominantly verbalisers, who can only sort out their thoughts when they speak aloud. One meets such people walking in the street. Others think by talking matters over quietly with themselves; and I have met many who daily exhaust themselves with incessant internal speech, carrying on conversations with themselves into the small hours, unable to sleep although physically worn out. They are creating their own stress, keeping the excitement in the nervous system above the threshold of sleep.

The whole output of nervous energy involved in a full ten-hour day of intense intellectual activity can be replaced by a small lump of sugar, so it is obvious that brainwork alone does not account for the worn-out businessman after a tiring day at the office, nor the exhausted university or schoolteacher towards the end of term. Fatigue comes from hard physical work, but also from excessive stress, brought about by the instinctive defensive muscular tensions developed in response to encountered stressors, and also through the incessant verbalisation and visualisation involved in mental processes. Once you have learned to manage your stress through differential muscular relaxation, you can get on with the job in hand without being exhausted at the end of the day.

Lesson 8: Relaxing the muscles of speech

If you have been practising the techniques set out in previous lessons, you must have made some progress towards managing your stress, otherwise it is hardly likely that you will still be reading this book. The new skills you have acquired should make it much easier for you to master lessons eight and nine, which are probably the most difficult, and perhaps the most rewarding. You will learn to relax the muscles of speech in the same way as before, by raising the perception of tension to the level of awareness, then letting the tension go. Seek a quiet place for your practice, which can be done sitting or lying in the basic position. In order to read the instructions you must have your eyes open, but once you have grasped what you have to do, close your eyes so that you can pay more attention to the 'T' signals from the muscles concerned.

1.   Put the fingertips of your left hand firmly on your throat, just above your larynx (Adam's apple). Now recite aloud in a clear speaking voice, the words of a short poem or a nursery rhyme. As you recite, notice carefully: the movements of your lips; the movements of your tongue; and the movements in your throat where your fingers are resting. As you are speaking loudly and clearly, there should be no difficulty in recognising these movements, which are due to muscle action. Let all these muscles relax.

2.   Now try again, this time speaking more quietly but deliberate-

ly, and again you will notice the tensions in the muscles of speech. Let them relax.

3.   Repeat the recitation, this time in a whisper. You will find the 'T' signals are diminished, but still present. Relax the muscles.

4.   After a few minutes rest, say the words into yourself, deliberately. It is likely that you will find the very slight movements of lips, tongue and throat still perceptible, showing that muscular action is still going on in these parts. Let the muscle relax.

5.   Without using your fingers (sense of touch), repeat the rhyme, and try to recognise the contractions taking place through the muscle sense alone. You may or may not be able to do so, for you may automatically have shifted from verbalisation to visualisation.

6.   Relax completely your lips, your tongue, your throat, and you will find that it is very difficult, or impossible, to speak to yourself. In other words, as you succeed in relaxing the various muscles of speech, there will be a quietening down of mental activity, at least as far as the verbalisation aspects are concerned.

This, however, is not the whole answer to those who wish to 'relax their minds'. In some, visualisation plays a more important part in thinking than does verbalisation. When an extreme visualiser is thinking a problem out, you can see his eyes moving about restlessly. 'Let me think, now', he says, and the eyeballs roll around in the sockets like balls in a pin-ball machine as he tries to pluck an elusive idea from his fickle memory, find a suitable phrase, or resolve a pressing problem. 'Shifty-eyed' is a pejorative term associated in novels with lower class, less intelligent characters, but it is, in fact, a trait found just as frequently in honourable, highly intelligent and educated individuals in any strata of society. This kind of thinking, where the thinker sees the words and situations which make up his thoughts, can be just as tiring and stressful as verbalising, for in both cases muscular activity is involved.

The eyeballs are moved by six small muscles which, if you have not learned to manage tension, rarely ever rest, even when you are asleep. The muscles are small, but their importance in stress management is enormous. Many subjects in whom this continuous eye movement is apparent report frequent headaches, and relief is experienced when they learn to relax their eye muscles. The stimuli coming from the eye muscles to the brain set up increased waves of electrical excitement in the nervous system, and this leads to tension in other muscle groups. The never-ending movement of the eyes, sweeping over a wide field, produces an increased input of visual stimuli, with further arousal.

From observation and discussion, I gain the impression that those who are visualisers learn more easily through the written word. Those who are predominantly verbalisers prefer the spoken word. It was mainly for the latter group that I produced in 1978 an audio-cassette on stress management that has proved popular in many countries. I do not yet understand how some become verbalisers, and others become visualisers, whether it is learned or inherited, but I am sure it has something to do with ability to learn in school, and later. Your own practice will be determined by what you find out about yourself. If you are primarily a verbaliser, place more emphasis on relaxing the muscles of speech; if a visualiser, practise relaxing your eyes.

Lesson 9: Relaxing your eye muscles
Check on the feeling of tension in your eyes in the following way, either sitting or lying down.

1. Close your eyes, and after a few seconds, try to look round towards your left ear. You will feel a strong tension in the left side of your eyes, as the muscles pull the eyeball across. Hold it for a few seconds, just to make sure you are getting the 'T' signals, then let your eyes return to the middle of the socket. After about half a minute, try to look at your right ear, and note the tension as you try to perform this impossible task. With a brief rest interval, try to look at your hair, and then at your chin, and in each case note the tension in the eye muscles. Then let your eyes return to the middle of the socket, so that all the muscles are relaxed . All this is only to help you to be aware of what eye tension feels like, and need never be repeated.
2. This is concerned with eye tensions in the thinking process. As you have to do the practice with your eyes closed, first read the paragraph carefully, so that you understand what you have to do. Relax the muscles of speech as completely as you can. Now think of the following numbers: 17, 19, 29, 37, 47. Close your eyes and add

them all together. What answer do you get – 139, 145, 149, 155, or 159? The answer is unimportant unless you are an A-type personality, but check your total again to make certain. Notice how, as you are working out the answer, the eye muscles contract slightly to move your eyes as you jump from one number to another. You may even find your outer eye muscles and your forehead muscles screwing up a little as well. In other words, you are using your muscles to think. If the figures given above are too easy for you, make up your own and try again.

3.   Keep the muscles of speech completely relaxed. Relax your eye muscles as much as you possibly can, keeping your eyes closed. Now try to add the figures together again, or subtract each in turn from the total you found. You will find that with your eye muscles relaxed, and your speech muscles relaxed, your thinking has become much more difficult. If they are completely relaxed, thinking is impossible.

4.   Try another kind of visualisation. Imagine a situation with which you are familiar – a room with several people in it, working, moving about, talking. In your imagination, follow the people about the room, out of the door, back in again, across the room. Look at the doorway; look at the window; look at the ceiling; and notice how, as you are picturing this scene, the eyes move with the changing figures in your imagination. Relax your eye muscles as completely as you can, and you will find that it is very difficult to visualise scenes like this, where movement is involved, or the object of your visualising is changing.

Once you have learned this technique of relaxing the eye muscles and the muscles of speech, you will find that it is not difficult to rest the mind at any time during the day or night, if you really want to do so.

STRESS AND INSOMNIA

When we encounter a stressful episode in our lives, acute or chronic, one of the first casualties is sleep. Removed from the stressor, but unable to put it out of our mind, we may lie, tossing and turning, triggering off the stress arousal again and again, retaining a high level of physiological activity, with the level of excitation in the nervous system never falling to the threshold necessary for sleep, until exhaustion sets in. Sleep is one of our essential needs, although the amount needed varies enormously from one individual to another.

If you cannot get off to sleep, it is because the level of excitement in the nervous system remains too high. You can quieten down the excitement in the nervous system, and diminish your level of stress by using the techniques you have already learned, relaxing your muscles, in particular, the muscles of speech and of visualisation.

Getting off to Sleep

1.   Lie in a comfortable position, on your back, your front or your side, and close your eyes.
2.   Let all the muscles of your body be relaxed – your face, hands and arms, shoulders, neck, upper back, lower back, abdomen, legs and feet – as you have already practised.
3.   Now let your speech muscles relax – tongue, lips, throat and jaw, so that you cannot speak to yourself.
4.   Let your eye muscles be completely relaxed, your eyes flopping down in the sockets, so that you cannot visualise. This can be difficult, as pictures keep flashing into your mind. So I suggest you follow a meditative technique. Meditation, in this sense, does not mean thinking about a particular topic. It means concentrating all the sensory apparatus on one particular stimulus, obliterating all the others. Use the skills that you learned in the first lesson of this book. Pay attention to the rhythm of your own breathing. Visualise, as it happens, the slight rise of your chest as you breathe in, the slight fall of your chest as you breathe out. Now and again you will suddenly find that you are visualising something different. Exclude this interruption, and bring your mind back again to visualising the rise and fall of your chest. There is a fair chance that you will soon be asleep. With practice, there is reasonable certainty that you will soon be asleep. If concentration on the rhythm of your breathing is not helpful for you, choose some other single stimulus – a word, a flower, etc., but not a scene, however beautiful. The latter is more likely to evoke further mental activity.

10
Growing Old Gracefully

To begin this final chapter with a well-worn cliché as title may leave me open to a charge of counselling perfection, and in a speculative manner. But clichés continue to exist simply because they express concepts in a meaningful way. Having arrived at my own seventieth year in a reasonable state of health after a full, exciting and interesting life, I can safely consider some of the factors which help one towards an enjoyable and rewarding senior citizenship. Stress is much the same amongst older people as amongst the younger. Scores on the PSTR Inventory show no significant differences between the under-twenties and the over-sixties. The stressors, however, may be somewhat different. Stressors with which we have battled for many years, such as promotion, recognition at work, or a growing family, are perceived differently. New stressors, including loneliness, loss of a sense of worth, financial difficulties, or failing health, may begin to impinge.

How we are able to cope with stress in old age depends to a very great extent on how we have coped at earlier ages. Throughout this book I have tried to argue that the way to manage your stress is through muscular relaxation in the presence of a stressor. This does not mean running away from life, or lying down on the floor, or seeking the comfort of an armchair or bed, or sitting cross-legged contemplating your navel. It means being relatively relaxed as you walk or talk or work or play, as you pursue your ambitions and achieve your goals. It is just as important when you retire as it was when wrestling with a job or a family.

THE BASES OF GOOD HEALTH

The state of your health (or wholeness) depends, at any stage of your life, on four sound bases. These are the physical, psychological, social and spiritual aspects of health. If, in earlier years, these bases are unsound, it may presage a host of difficulties and stress ahead. While we are still young, it is relatively easy to overcome the handicaps of earlier life. It becomes more difficult to do this as we grow older, but by no means impossible.

Physical Needs

The physical basis of good health in later years is composed of sound diet, moderate exercise, some form of work that makes demands upon your skills, and adequate rest. Don't be misled by the multitude of fashionable diets spewed out weekly by newspapers and magazines. If they had it right the first time, they wouldn't have to keep changing it every week. Continue to eat the things you have liked to eat, but not quite so much. In this way, you are likely to gain all the energy foods, the building foods, the fats, minerals and vitamins that you need. In particular, eat fibre-rich foods to help keep your digestive system in good working order, and go easy on the salt. For exercise, to maintain the heart and lungs in good condition, frequent walking is adequate, or you may choose to play golf or bowls, or join dancing classes or exercise groups for the social spin-off, sharing your fun with others. Exercise has wonderful psychological benefits as well as physical benefits.

As for work, if you've just given it up you might not like the sound of the word at all. If your work has been your life, and you have been unwillingly retired, you may find yourself greatly stressed by having it no longer. Then you must find something to do, using your existing skills or developing new skills, doing it to earn a little more, or doing it as a hobby, entirely voluntarily. Your health requires that you do something that is meaningful and purposeful for you, even if others may regard it as eccentric. You can work as hard as you like, provided that you also take adequate rest, whether this means sleeping soundly at night, or having a rest period and maybe a nap during the day. Work helps you to sleep; reasonable sleep helps you to work. In this way, the physical aspect of your stress management is well maintained.

Psychological Needs

The psychological needs of individuals do not change very much in the course of life. Failure, for one reason or another, to meet these needs is a major cause of stress at any age. The main needs are love, acceptance, understanding, recognition, order, freedom, and independence. Except for love, we can tolerate non-fulfilment of these needs for varying periods but, knowingly or unknowingly, we are seeking to satisfy them for most of our lives.

Love is the most important of all psychological needs. To be loved and to love are the most potent forces in human life and interaction. Loss of love or loss of a loved person, is the most common cause of stress, and of stress-related illness, far outstripping anything else that happens in life as a stressor. Withdrawal of love is a painful punishment meted out to children by parents or by spouses to one another, or friend to friend. Love is often debased, euphemistically equating fornication with 'making love', when so often it is making hatred, or just using another person for self-gratification. A recent popular song contained the line, 'The joys of love are fleeting . . . ', but, indeed, they are not. They last forever.

It is relatively easy to love our parents or our children, our brothers or sisters, and our chosen mates. This is a conditioned reflex, strengthened by every loving interaction, or diminished by lack of loving interaction. Loving our neighbours, people we may not know, is not so easy, but it is equally important for the welfare of mankind. Loving our neighbours – that is, being concerned for their welfare – is not a conditioned reflex. It is a logical, intellectual act of the will. It is peculiarly human, and is essential in the management of stress. There are those who deeply love and strive for their own families, but by their actions, in business, in politics, in religion and in sex, destroy other people's parents and children, sowing widespread, without love, without pity, the stress that brings destruction and death in human affairs. It matters not whether you believe in a loving God as the motivation in loving your neighbour. If you are not concerned for the welfare of others in the solution of human stress, then you remain part of the problem. If you learn to love those who work beside you, or live next door, you will also diminish stress in the farthest corners of the world. If you are concerned for the health and welfare of those in distant lands, but spurn those who live around you, you remain one of the stressors of the world.

All the exercises, the relaxation practices, the meditations, the therapies, the counsellings, the stress management courses (including my own) are in vain, if you cannot give love to, and receive love from, your fellow beings. In this, as Scrooge found out for himself, you must be the prime mover.

We are social animals, and we seek *acceptance* in one group or another. When we are rejected, we experience stress, and will seek out another group, orthodox, bizarre, or revolutionary, where we will be accepted, or withdraw into destructive reclusion. We hope for *understanding* from others for our personal idiosyncratic behaviour, and will strive or deceive to find it ('My wife does not really understand me, but you, my dear . . . '). We need *recognition* for our achievements, through a kind word, a hug, a pat on the back, a promotion, election to a Royal Society, a critic's praise, or merely a word of thanks. We are all subject to criticism in the work that we do, and it spurs us on to greater effort. But constant criticism of our work, at home or in our occupation, with no rewarding recognition, destroys initiative, restricts effort, and creates a lot of stress. The carping boss, the grumbling husband, and the nagging wife have much to answer for. We can live with disorder and indiscipline in our lives for a time, but a surfeit is likely to produce much stress. The need for *order* (or *discipline*) in human affairs will assert itself.

Men and women become sick, and fight or die to achieve *freedom* and *independence*, whether of the personal or national variety. When it is absent, stress may be pervasive and crippling, or a motive to action. All these needs are reciprocal. If you freely help to satisfy them in others, they are returned to you in abundance, and in the few situations where this may not happen, you do not experience stress. If you carelessly or deliberately withhold satisfaction of these needs from others, you cannot hope to find them satisfied in yourself, and inevitably, you will experience more stress.

Social Needs

Some people have difficulty in making and keeping friends. Maybe it's because somewhere along the growing process they missed out

94

on some of Erikson's 'senses', and have never reached the integrity stage. Maybe they say they are quite self-sufficient, and don't need anybody else. But social support is very important in managing stress, and in alleviating anxiety. Stay friendly with your friends, so that they enjoy having you around. Follow the advice of Polonius to his son Laertes:

'Those friends thou hast, and their adoption tried,
Grapple them to thy soul with hoops of steel.'

To be able to laugh with friends, and at friends, in mutual joy, is one of the great privileges of life. It can quickly reduce events perceived as threatening to the absurdities that they so often are. In real emergencies, you are more likely to have the help that you need.

Many have to live alone in later years, because of loss of spouse, or mobility of children, or other reasons. Make your own social life by finding out organisations that interest you, and meeting people with whom you can work at shared tasks. It may be paid work or voluntary work, helping people who are older, needier or more handicapped than yourself. Talk with people, instead of sitting around waiting for people to talk with you. Nice as it is to have some peace and quiet at times, isolation is a major stressor, but it is usually a circumstance you can circumvent by your own efforts.

Spiritual Needs

Frequently, when I have been conducting workshops on stress management, someone will come up to me at the end of the session, and say, 'That was fine, but you said nothing about the spiritual needs, about the value of religious belief in reducing or managing stress.' True, I usually don't, unless I am working with religious groups. That religious belief and religious practice can have a very important part to play in managing stress, I have no doubt whatsoever. It is important in my own life. But it is readily recognised that religious belief and practice can at times be severe stressors, for believers and unbelievers alike.

As we grow older, it is important to have a belief, a philosophy which guides us in our lives. It is necessary to give purpose and meaning to what we do, against which we can readily measure and evaluate the stressors we encounter. If we hold fast to it, we are less likely to be blown about by every philosophical wind that becomes fashionable, more likely to perceive stressors for the impostors they so often are, and to act accordingly. How long we live is not very important, if life is miserable. Through sensible management of our stress, we can ensure that the quality of our living is good throughout the only life we have with which to experiment.

Lesson 10: Living with stress

This is the last and the longest lesson in the book, for it lasts for the rest of your life. If you have practised the lessons in the previous chapters, you will have gone some way towards improving your skill in managing your own stress. Few of us ever acquire a psychomotor skill perfectly. So continue to practise, at times away from any stress situation, and at other times, in actual stress situations. Apply what you have learned in every potential stress encounter, afterwards assessing your success. Sometimes you will fail; other times you will succeed. Each time you succeed in controlling your own stress level will give you more confidence for the next encounter.

No one else can do it for you, but now you know that through your own efforts, you can manage your stress. When you do so, your whole life will be much more rewarding.

Note   A cassette, Live Well with Stress and Tension, is available from Macdonald Wallace Associates, Health Education Consultants, 14 Cranleigh Avenue, Rottingdean, East Sussex, England.